Contents

Spring Persistence: *A Running Start*

by Paul Tepper Fisher and Solomon Duskis

This book has been in the making for a couple of years. The journey began when we had the revelation that, despite Spring's growing popularity, few books were available that really focused on persistence. Every day, software developers overcome obstacles, extracting valuable lessons from their experiences. Since so much development centers on the topic of persisting and retrieving data, we decided to write a book that would serve to relay some of the enriching experiences and lessons we have accumulated over the years through development with Spring and the myriad persistence technologies available today.

Our aim is to create a valuable resource, a guidebook of sorts, to help developers become better acquainted with Spring and some of the most popular persistence frameworks currently available. It is not our intention for this book to serve as yet another Spring reference. Rather, these chapters are intended to share lessons and experiences, as well as proven design patterns, for developing scalable applications using the Spring Framework.

Our approach throughout each chapter of this book is to chronicle the development process for building a layered persistence tier using Spring. Each chapter builds on the previous one to introduce a different persistence technology using integration best practices for Spring. Our sample application follows the implementation of an art gallery slideshow. Through example and discussion, we trace the steps required to design, architect, and implement this web-based application, demonstrating foundational Spring concepts and strategies along the way.

Writing this book has been a journey both educational and rewarding. Many of the ideas and approaches discussed in this book originate from our own development experiences and lessons. We cover a lot of ground, including basic and advanced concepts, and we hope that this book will impart useful strategies and patterns that you can apply to your next project.

Acknowledgements

Writing a book is never the result of a single person's efforts. It requires the support and encouragement of others. This project could never have been realized without the unwavering patience of Melanie Colton, to whom I dedicate this book. A lot of long, sleep-deprived nights went into this project, and she's kept me (marginally) sane for the duration. I also would like to acknowledge my colleagues at Wired.com and CondéNet for all of their patience and support over the years. I'd especially like to thank Rajiv Pant and Evan Hansen for their guidance, trust, and mentorship.

Solomon Duskis made this project possible by making the case for a book on Spring persistence and inspiring us to embark on this adventure. There are few people as passionate and dedicated to their work as Solomon, with whom it has been an honor and a privilege to work on this project.

Finally, we can't thank Apress enough for all of their guidance and support over the last few months. Heather Lang and Sofia Marchant have been unbelievably patient with us throughout this process and have been helpful every step of the way. And thanks to Steve Anglin for believing in us and championing our book to Apress. It's been an absolute pleasure working with everyone at Apress, and we look forward to starting our next book, Spring Persistence: The Sequel.

Paul Tepper Fisher

My wife of ten years, Riki, and my kids have been extremely patient through this. I couldn't have finished this book without them all listening to my ideas and giving me time and encouragement. I do have to acknowledge that this book would not have been finished if not for Paul Fisher. His perseverance, knowledge, and late nights went well beyond the call of duty. Last, but not least, I would like to thank my SunGard colleagues Kevin, Neil, and Dave for their support and faith throughout the last couple of years as I wrote this book.

Solomon Duskis

Chapter 1: Introducing Spring Persistence

Long-term persistence of information is the key component of most enterprise systems. The Spring Framework's ability to seamlessly integrate with myriad persistence frameworks has helped to make it one of the most popular frameworks for building robust, scalable applications. At the simplest level, Spring is a lightweight Inversion of Control (IoC) container, meaning Spring will take over the responsibility of wiring together your application dependencies; the manner in which this wiring responsibility is handled is most important. However, the theme you will see played out in this book is the way that Spring effortlessly ties components together in a loosely coupled manner. This goal has far-reaching effects for any application, as it allows code to be more easily refactored and maintained. And in the context of this book, it allows developers to build a persistence tier that is not directly tied to a particular implementation or framework. Not only does this agnostic persistence tier lead to better, cleaner code, it also ensures consistency across your application. Suddenly, your code is supported by a cohesive backbone, as well as having a centralized configuration that implicitly documents the way your application's pieces fit together.

In this chapter, we will cover some of the foundational concepts of the Spring Framework and how they can be applied to integrate Spring and your persistence framework of choice into your application. We will also cover some of the core design patterns and strategies that a Spring-based application should follow. These design patterns and strategies will be discussed throughout this book and will form the basis of our examples in later chapters.

Persistence

Persistence. Sometimes, it's the only way to get the girl. Sometimes, it leads to a restraining order, and sometimes, restraining orders can lead to stalking charges even when you specifically carry around measuring tape to *prove* that you are never less than 15 feet away. But this book is not really about restraining orders; in fact, that's an entirely different book, soon to be adapted into a made-for-TV movie. This book is about a different kind of persistence altogether, the kind of persistence that nearly every software application requires as part of its *modus operandi*. Persistence can be defined as a process that allows data to continue to exist—even outside its originating process. Essentially, persistence is what often makes a program truly practical, allowing it to maintain data and application state for longer than a single request or invocation. It provides the core foundation on which business logic can do its thing, usually performing further data analysis and manipulation.

Until recently, data persistence could be a very laborious task, often with little room for flexibility. In most cases, persistence implies interaction with a relational database, but as you'll learn in later chapters, this isn't always the case, at least not directly. Here is where the Spring Framework comes in: Spring makes integrating different persistent strategies into your application easy; you can even switch among alternate databases or other persistence technologies. However, understanding Spring is only half the battle. It is also important to comprehend how these persistence frameworks work, how they differ, and how they interface with your code.

This book will cover a lot of what you need to know about how to effectively use Spring together with your persistence framework of choice. We'll start with the basics, working directly with a database via straight JDBC and then demonstrate how Spring's JDBC support can drastically simplify the way your application communicates with a database, even minimizing more mundane nuances, such as connection details and configuration. We'll then move onto object-relational mapping (ORM) frameworks, so you'll better understand how object-relational technologies can significantly speed up application development (and even improve performance). We'll start with the basic concepts and then cover some of the more popular implementations, including Hibernate, Java Persistence API (JPA), iBATIS, Java Content Repository (JCR), and Grails, demonstrating the benefits of using domain-based persistence solutions that abstract lower level database concepts away from your application.

The more your code is abstracted away from interfacing directly with a database (and dealing with the lower level concerns), the easier it is to switch to a different database or persistence technology. Spring centralizes the wiring of dependencies within your application, making maintenance and configuration easier and coercing developers to code to interfaces, which brings about cleaner and better code. It also allows you to focus more on your application's business logic, with less concern over how this information is physically stored and retrieved. This concept is often called *layering*: each layer should be focused specifically on accomplishing a particular task (with little knowledge of or coupling to other layers within the application). The layer that deals with persistence is often called the *persistence layer*, while the layer that handles the business logic is (surprisingly enough) called the *service layer*. As you'll see in later chapters, this separation of concerns helps keep your code clean and ensures that details from one layer don't meddle with the code from another layer. When it comes time for refactoring, this advantage can be significant.

This book will also cover some more advanced persistence concepts that are indispensable in most applications, such as database transactions and optimization techniques for loading and managing complex relationships and collections within your domain model. We will also discuss performance strategies, such as caching at both the domain level and higher abstractions.

Part of Spring's momentum comes from the way it enables applications to deliver enterprise-level features, such as declarative transactions and security, without requiring the overhead and complexity of an Enterprise JavaBean (EJB) container or the need to master details specific to a technology or standard. Time has proven EJB, although powerful in theory, to be a victim of overengineering. Much of Spring's success stems from the Java community's need for a framework that delivers enterprise-level features without the tremendous overhead and learning curve required by the EJB standard. Spring was built and popularized by this growing need to fill the void that EJB left behind. With the Spring Framework's success came a stronger emphasis on building applications that were simpler and lighter weight, which significantly impacts both the ease of maintenance and capacity to scale an application.

Spring as a de Facto Standard

Despite what some may claim, the Spring Framework is not currently a standard. Standard technologies are great, and I give Sun a gold star for pushing standards-based technologies into the mainstream. Standards allow you to develop your web application on Tomcat and then drop it into WebSphere with little adjustment required (at least theoretically). But even though the Spring Framework is unbelievably popular today, it does not represent a true standard; some consider it a *de facto standard*, due to the sheer volume of applications that rely on it. Nevertheless, Spring does provide a means for integrating the various components of your application in a consistent way and is deployed far and wide across a variety of application ecosystems. Sometimes, this type of *standard implementation* is a far more valuable proposition than a *standard specification*. Despite the naysayers that balk at the idea of using any technology that wasn't designed by a giant committee of corporate volunteers, I think using Spring in your application poses little risk. In fact, the more you utilize Spring for integrating components into your application, the more consistent your integration strategy will be, making maintenance and development easier. That's right: reliance on Spring will often lead to better, cleaner, decoupled code.

Spring and JavaBeans

Part of what accelerated Spring's adoption was its reliance on several foundational patterns and concepts that had been kicked around in the Java world for quite some time. One of these concepts is known as the JavaBean. The JavaBean is little more than a standard Java class, often called a plain old Java object (POJO) that follows some simple rules:

- It has a public, default constructor.

- It contains public getters and setters for each property that is to be read or written respectively (write permissions can be obscured simply by defining a getter and no setter).

The JavaBean concept was originally devised for Swing to facilitate the development of stand-alone GUI components, but the pattern has been repurposed for the land of Spring beans and, in our case, backend persistence. Although frighteningly simple, Spring's use of the JavaBean as a means of configuration and integration is quite powerful. Consider the example of a ValidUser bean, which could be utilized in an application to specify user credential information:

```
<bean id="validUserOne"
    class="com.dialmercury.apress.ValidUser">
    <property name="username" value="paul" />
    <property name="password" value="foo" />
</bean>
```

You can take away several things from the preceding example. The first is that I use horribly insecure passwords (my luggage is even worse). But more importantly, we learn how a simple Spring bean is configured via XML. To make this work on the Java side, we need a valid JavaBean class that looks like the following:

```
package com.dialmercury.apress

class ValidUser {
 private String username;
 private String password;
  public ValidUser() {}

  public String getUsername() {
    return this.username;
  }

  public void setUsername(String name) {
    this.username = name;
  }

  public String getPassword() {
    return this.password;
  }

  public void setPassword(password) {
    this.password = password;
  }
 }
}
```

Notice that, for each property entity in the Spring XML configuration, we have a corresponding getter and setter defined in the Java class. In Spring terms, this is called *setter injection*, since the property values are configured by invoking the JavaBean's setter methods. An alternate approach is to use *constructor injection*, which allows the property values to be injected via the constructor of the class. To use constructor injection, we would refactor our code and Spring configuration as follows:

```
<bean id="validUserOne"
    class="com.dialmercury.apress.ValidUser">
    <constructor-arg index="0" value="paul" />
    <constructor-arg index="1" value="foo" />
</bean>
```

```
package com.dialmercury.apress

class ValidUser {
  private String username;
  private String password;
   public ValidUser(String username, String password) {
     this.username = username;
     this.password = password;
  }

  public String getUsername() {
    return this.username;
  }


  public String getPassword() {
    return this.password;
  }
 }
}
```

Although either approach is valid, we recommend the setter-based approach, as this better conforms to the JavaBean principles and makes your code easier to test later.

In the preceding example, you'll notice that we injected two string values, which are specified directly within the configuration file. This is a useful shortcut to abstract basic configuration details away from your code and into a more readily changeable file. However, the same concept can be taken a step further for satisfying dependencies between collaborating instances within your application. For example, suppose you have a class designed to handle a portion of the persistence-specific functionality in your application and another web application controller class that delegates to this first class for loading and saving application behavior. In your Spring configuration file, you might have the following:

```
<bean id="galleryManager"
  class="com.dialmercury.apress.GalleryManager">
  <property name="personDao><ref bean="personDao"/>
</bean>

<bean id="personDao"
  class="com.dialmercury.apress.HibernatePersonDao">
    <property name="sessionFactory"
      ref="hibernateSessionFactory"/>
</bean>
```

Simple, isn't it? We just wired up critical parts of our application with a few lines of configuration.

Earlier, we mentioned that Spring has the tendency to lead developers to write better, cleaner, and more loosely coupled code. You might be starting to pick up on why this is the case: not only are your classes free of application wiring code, applications based on Spring are usually more interface based, meaning that your code is dependent on interfaces rather than specific implementations. This strategy is often called *coding to interfaces*, and it allows us to easily swap out one implementation for another, simply by altering the class attribute within a Spring bean. As long as your code is written to rely on an interface, no changes to your class files will be necessary.

For instance, notice that in the preceding example, the `galleryManager` bean depends on a `personDao` bean. In your code, a good practice is to define a `PersonDao` interface that specifies core data access methods related to user access and security. As an oversimplified example, our `PersonDao` interface might look like the following:

```
public interface PersonDao {
    public Person getPerson(Long personId) ;
    public void savePerson(Person person) ;
    public List<Person> getPeople() ;
    public Person getPersonByUsername(String username)
      throws EntityNotFoundException ;
```

```
      public Person authenticatePerson(
         String username, String password)
         throws AuthenticationException ;
   }
```

The personDao bean would then specify a class attribute that points to a particular implementation of the PersonDao interface. In the preceding spring configuration example, the implementation is written to use Hibernate (hence "Hibernate" in the class name HibernatePersonDao). But we could just as easily have written a JDBC-based PersonDao , or even a Mock-PersonDao, implementation utilized for unit testing our GalleryManager class. The key point here is that the GalleryManager class does not depend directly on the HibernatePersonDao implementation but rather depends on the PersonDao interface. Although the difference may appear subtle, expressing dependencies on interfaces is an effective means of ensuring your application is loosely coupled. If your code doesn't express any direct coupling to a particular implementation, you will gain the flexibility of defining these details in the Spring configuration and only that configuration. In this way, you can easily swap implementations (for instance, switch from a HibernatePersonDao to a JdbcPersonDao) without having to refactor your code. You will see later how interface-driven code and Spring will make unit testing and mocking easy.

No matter what type of library, class, or framework you need to integrate into your application, Spring will allow you to work with these internal and external components cleanly and with a shallow learning curve. This integration without direct coupling is the greatest benefit IoC. Essentially, the hooks into third-party libraries (or even in-house frameworks and classes) are moved outside the source code and into configuration files (or annotation-based metadata within your classes). This type of configuration lets developers worry less about how the various components of code fit together and focus more on coding the core functionality itself.

Inversion of Control and Dependency Injection

IoC is a very powerful concept and represents the foundation on which the Spring Framework is based. The ability to externalize simple class properties is just the beginning; with Spring, developers can create a complex tree of dependencies, leaving the work of figuring out how each dependency is created and set (also called *injected* or *wired*) to the Spring lightweight container.

Another type of injection is what Spring calls *autowiring*. This method allows you to simply define setters and getters of a particular type or name, putting on the Spring container the onus of figuring out which class to inject. This very powerful feature comes with some risk as well—should there be some ambiguity as to which instance to inject, you may run into problems. For instance, if you have a class that depends on the PersonDao interface and you have both a HibernatePersonDao and a JDBCPersonDao defined in your application (both of which implement the PersonDao interface), Spring may get confused as to which implementation you intend to inject.

Beginning with Spring 2.5, another configuration strategy was introduced. Utilizing annotation-based metadata, you can now specify dependency wiring directly within your classes. The advantage of this approach is that a class's dependencies can be expressed directly within the code. The downside to this strategy is that you don't benefit from having a centralized collection of configuration files that illustrate and document how your application's components are wired. The path you take is up to you, and certainly, using annotations does simplify the configuration process. Furthermore, you can certainly mix and match both XML configuration and annotations, allowing certain dependencies to be configured within the Spring XML, while other dependencies are detected via annotations.

As an example, let's take a look at our simple PersonDao using an annotation-based approach.

We haven't actually defined our `PersonDao` implementation yet, so let's do that now. In this example, we'll define our Hibernate implementation. Notice that the `HibernatePersonDaoImpl` implements the `PersonDao` interface we introduced earlier:

```
@Repository("personDao")
public class HibernatePersonDaoImpl
   extends HibernateDaoSupport
   implements PersonDao {

   @Autowired
   public void setupSessionFactory(
     SessionFactory sessionFactory) {
        this.setSessionFactory(sessionFactory);
   }

   public Person getPerson(Long personId)
     throws DataAccessException {
        return (Person) this.getHibernateTemplate()
          .load(Person.class, personId);
   }
 ...(Methods omitted)
 }
```

There are a few details to take away from this example. First, is the `@Repository` annotation. Spring defines three core stereotype annotations, each of which represents a layer within a typical application: `@Repository`, `@Controller`, and `@Service`.

`@Repository` is used to delineate those classes that serve as an interface with a data repository. In this case, it is our Data Access Object (DAO) implementation, as it serves the purpose of abstracting all data access functionality that relate to the `Person` domain object.

The `@Controller` annotation is used to delineate controller classes, which are used in the web layer to handle requests.

Last, the `@Service` annotation defines a service facade. Typically, the service layer wraps the DAO layer, providing a coherent, transactional service that often serves as the business logic for an application (we will discuss the service layer further in later chapters). The service layer is often called a facade, since it serves as an abstraction over the data-access code, hiding the lower level implementation details and providing a business-specific API.

These three annotations logically extend from the `@Component` annotation, which defines any bean intended to be managed by the Spring container.

Next, you'll notice the `@Autowired` annotation above the `setupSessionFactory()` method. This tells Spring to inject (using the autowiring strategy we discussed earlier) an implementation of the `SessionFactory` interface. In cases where ambiguity could be an issue, Spring provides a means for providing clues to the container by using qualifiers. *Qualifiers* can be inserted within an XML configuration to provide specific hints to the Spring container in order to help disambiguate a situation in which multiple instances of a particular type or interface are present. For instance, if we were using multiple datasources and multiple Hibernate `SessionFactory` interfaces, we might indicate which `SessionFactory` was needed by adding the following annotation:

```
    @Autowired
    @Qualifier("userSessionFactory")
  public void setupSessionFactory(
    SessionFactory sessionFactory) {
       this.setSessionFactory(sessionFactory);
  }
```

In the XML configuration, we might have this:

```
  <bean id="sessionFactory"
    class="org.springframework.orm.hibernate3. ⮞
    annotation. AnnotationSessionFactoryBean"
```

```
    p:dataSource-ref="dataSource"
    p:lobHandler-ref="defaultLobHandler">
      <qualifier value="userSessionFactory"/>
 …(Configuration omitted)
  </bean>
```

It is also important to point out that the `@Autowired` annotation may be applied to more than just setters. It can also be applied to methods and constructors. Furthermore, the `@Qualifier` annotation may be applied directly to method parameters to target qualification to a specific parameter or to apply different qualifying hints to different parameters within a method or constructor.

Exploring Spring Design Patterns and Strategies

All this externalization doesn't seem like a big deal at first, but it really is, and you'll notice that when you begin development. You can simply focus on the implementation without worrying about how a reference from one class can get to another. You learn to simply define setters and getters for the dependencies each class requires, and then leave the wiring to Spring.

Imagine some of the alternatives. Many applications rely on singletons to centralize and hand out references to needed dependencies. This type of strategy will certainly work, but inevitably, your code becomes more about wiring classes together than about your application's core functionality. Spring and IoC allow you to focus on the application design and business logic and forget about the wiring. I remember Ron Popeil's Showtime Rotisserie advertisement's tagline, "Set it, and forget it!" I find this slogan floating through my head each time I start developing with Spring.

The Spring Life Cycle

Spring not only instantiates objects and wires up dependencies but also handles each managed object's *life cycle*. For example, what if you need to do some initialization in your class, after the Spring-injected properties have been set? One way to accomplish this is through constructor injection (so that you can capture the moment all of a bean's properties are injected). But a cleaner approach is to use the `init-method` feature. By defining an `init-method` attribute on your bean, you can specify an arbitrary method that will get called after all of the Spring properties have been set (that is, after all of your setters have been invoked). Here is an example of using the `init-method` feature of Spring:

```
<bean id="initTest"
  class="com.dialmercury.apress.InitTest"
  init-method="init">
    <property name="testString"
      value="Let me out of this computer!"/>
</bean>
```

Simple, right? Next, we need to define a class with the `init-method`, we specified in the preceding configuration:

```
package com.dialmercury.apress

class InitTest {
  private String testString;

  public void init() {
    //let's do some initialization stuff!
    if (this.getTestString() == null) {
      throw new RuntimeException(
        "Hey, man, you forgot to set the ➥
testString property! What were you thinking???";
    }
  }

  public void setTestString(String testString) {
    this.testString = testString;
  }

  public String getTestString() {
```

```
      return this.testString;
    }
  }
```

If you're using Java 5 or greater, you can also tap into Spring's annotation support for initialization and destruction events. Using this approach, you simply annotate a class's methods with the `@postConstruct` or `@preDestroy` annotation. For example, we could refactor our earlier example as follows:

```
package com.dialmercury.apress

class InitTest {
  private String testString;

  @PostConstruct()
  public void init() {
    //let's do some initialization stuff!
    if (this.getTestString() == null) {
      throw new RuntimeException(
        "Hey, man, you forgot to set the ➥
  testString property! What were you thinking???";
    }
    ...(Methods omitted)
  }
```

As with everything in Spring, there's actually more than one way to skin a cat. (We do not condone the act of skinning a cat or any other animal for that matter. In fact, we shouldn't have even used that metaphor, and we assert that no animals have been hurt during the writing of this book.) Instead of specifying `init-method` in the configuration, you could instead have your class implement the `InitializingBean` interface. To a certain extent, using this interface makes things a bit easier, since you don't even need to change your configuration. The interface just requires you to implement an `afterPropertiesSet()` method, which will automatically get detected and called for you once Spring has finished setting all the configured properties. The downside, however, is that this approach couples your application to Spring. And even though coupling to Spring isn't such a bad thing, the cleaner approach is to keep initialization details entirely within configuration and out of the code. So let this be your mantra: keep it in the configuration.

An Overview of Handy Spring Interfaces

Spring does support a range of beneficial interfaces that your class *can* implement. For example, implementing `ApplicationContextAware` will ensure that your class has a reference to the Spring `applicationContext` bean (essentially the entity that configures and tracks all the beans configured through Spring). This interface has the following method:

```
void setApplicationContext(
  ApplicationContext appContext);
```

With access to Spring's `ApplicationContext` interface, your class has the flexibility to look up beans by name or type, as well as publish events (to which other classes can subscribe). We will cover some of these more advanced Spring features in later in this chapter.

Another neat interface is `DisposableBean`, which is essentially the inverse of `InitializingBean`, allowing you to handle the event in which a bean is destroyed (also accomplished via configuration using the `destroy-method` parameter).

If you are running on Java 5 or greater, you can also use annotations to specify initialization or destroy methods directly in your Java code.

Slick configuration and life cycle management are really only a small portion of the overall Spring package. Spring also provides powerful integration points to myriad frameworks, including a handful of persistence frameworks, greatly simplifying the integration of these frameworks into an application and making maintenance and development easier overall.

We will cover some of the most popular of these integration hooks in the next few chapters.

Beyond these integration points, Spring also provides a powerful set of Aspect-Oriented Programming (AOP) and proxying features, which are instrumental for configuring declarative transactions, logging, and remoting—capabilities that make Spring a viable replacement for the enterprise-level features offered by EJB and Java Enterprise Edition (JEE) application servers.

Injecting Code Using AOP and Interceptors

AOP is often a hard pill for developers to swallow. In truth, it can be a somewhat confusing topic, as it is a fairly new development paradigm, and for those experienced in object-oriented methodologies, AOP can seem a bit unconventional.

I often like to think of AOP as code injection. In much the same way that Spring provides a means to inject values and instance references into a bean, AOP allows developers to essentially weave code from one class directly into another. Why on Earth would you ever want to do this? Well, sometimes, you want to apply functionality across a whole slew of classes, but extending from a base class to accomplish this goal doesn't make sense, as the functionality you wish to inject may be *orthogonal* (that is, completely independent of or unrelated) to the destination class. This notion is often called *cross-cutting concerns*, because the intention with AOP is to apply functionality across a series of classes that has little to do with the classes' main purpose.

For example, say you have a few classes that are designed to store and retrieve data related to an image gallery. As part of this implementation, you may wish to do some auditing (for example, to track details of each successive write operation). Extending from a base auditing class isn't a viable or proper way to accomplish this task. You have one chance at concrete inheritance, and you probably don't want to waste it by inheriting the auditing behavior. If you extend from any class at all, you'd probably want to inherit behavior that relates more to manipulating your domain model and saving data related to the images in your gallery.

In this example, we might say that auditing functionality is orthogonal to the core image gallery functionality. Furthermore, the auditing aspects of the code can be applied in a reasonably similar and standard fashion across all the application code. This is the perfect scenario for AOP: you can apply aspects of the unrelated auditing functionality across all of the classes that aim to handle image gallery logic.

Code Weaving to Inject Functionality

The way this works in practice is fairly simple: a class's methods can be altered so that new functionality can be injected before, after, or around (essentially, before and after) a method is called. So, in the case of an auditing aspect, you could inject a block of code that writes a row in a database (constituting a piece of an overall auditing trail) each time a method within a category of methods is called. A similar scenario concerns security: a security check can be inserted into your core data-access code to ensure appropriate permissions or roles are verified each time certain methods are called. The interesting part of this concept is that you can keep the security aspects entirely separate from your core implementation (which no longer has to worry about the implementation details of security). Separating concerns leads to cleaner code, as your core application need not worry about the mundane details of security. These two distinct pieces of functionality can be developed and maintained entirely separately, leading to cleaner, decoupled architecture.

Now that you have a loosely coupled code base, you somehow need those different pieces to get recomposed so that your runtime behavior takes advantage of the right aspects at the right time. For example, the data-access code does need a security check. Those various aspects of the code get put back together in a process called *code weaving*.

Code weaving can happen at compile time, load time, and runtime. Each point in time has a different level of implementation complexity, different impacts on how quickly your code will run, and different limitations.

Spring accomplishes AOP with runtime code weaving through the use of the proxy design pattern: when you advise your classes, by injecting cross-cutting behavior into various methods, you're not actually injecting code at all. Rather, you're requesting that Spring create a new *proxy class*, in which functionality is delegated to your existing class along with the transactional implementation (or whatever aspect you are trying to weave into your code). This explanation is an oversimplification of what actually happens under the hood, but the important thing to remember is that when you inject behavior into your classes via AOP, Spring is not actually injecting code; it is replacing your class with a proxied class that has your existing code and the transactional code intertwined. Again, it's easy to see how this is a natural fit for a lightweight, IoC container like Spring. Since you're already entrusting Spring with handling your dependencies, it makes perfect sense to let Spring also take care of proxying these dependencies so you can layer on new, cross-cutting behavior.

In our security check example we discussed a few paragraphs ago, a Spring proxy will get called before any data access occurs. The proxy will call the security check and will call the data-access method only if the security check completes successfully.

Pointcuts are another important component of Spring AOP; they help to define where a particular *aspect* (injected functionality, such as committing a transaction) should be weaved into the targeted class.

Although Spring AOP is amazingly powerful when you need to define and introduce new aspects to be weaved into your implementations, key functionality is available out of the box and without the need to learn the details of AOP programming concepts. Declarative transaction support is probably the most common use of Spring AOP.

Using Declarative Transactions

This ability to intercept method calls and introduce, or inject, new functionality is the secret sauce behind Spring's support for declarative transactions. Using Spring's declarative transaction support, you can advise your persistence facade layer (which we will describe soon) with transactional semantics.

Note   *Transactional semantics* is a fancy way of saying that developers can put the transactional details inside a configuration file instead of muddling up the code. Using the word *semantics* will give you credibility in nearly any conversation; try it on your friends and watch them get flustered and intimidated. Then, when they look most sheepish, kick them in the shins: you're guaranteed to catch even the most guarded people by surprise.

Transactions define how and when data is committed to a database; they are indispensable in grouping persistence logic together, ensuring that all methods complete successfully or that the database is rolled back to its previous state. Transactional semantics are defined entirely in the Spring configuration. Prior to Spring, this capability was one of the primary benefits to using EJB, so the ability to externalize transactional details in a configuration without requiring the overhead of an EJB container is a powerful concept.

The service layer, which we'll talk about soon, is where Spring's AOP support is best utilized. Spring ships with transactional support in the form of interceptors that enhance your service layer code, by weaving in the transactional goodness. But it's not enough to simply specify that a method should be transactional. You shouldn't just force each method to occur within the confines of a transaction, rolling back if an error occurs and committing if all goes well. Perhaps certain methods don't need to occur within a transactional context at all. Or more likely, perhaps some exceptions will trigger a rollback, while others will allow the transaction to carry on. With Spring's transactional support, you have fine-grained control over what exceptions may trigger a commit or rollback, as well as the details over the transaction itself, such as determining the isolation level and whether a method should trigger a new transaction or a nested transaction or execute within the existing transaction.

We will come back to configuring declarative transactions in Spring soon. First, let's begin building our project's persistence tier, which will be composed of our domain model, DAO, and service facade.

Application Layering

We've found that developing the middle tier of an application in Spring is best served by following convention. Spring helps to enforce a modular architecture in which an application is divided into several core layers:

- Domain model
- Persistence Layer/DAOs
- Service layer/service facade
- Controllers

Each of these layers is representative of proven design patterns that are key to building a solid, maintainable architecture. No matter what persistence framework you choose, we recommend using a clean, layered approach for your persistence implementation. Spring encourages the use of DAOs; in fact, it has a variety of classes that make implementing the DAO pattern a snap.

Let's walk through the domain model, DAO, and service layers, step by step. Although controllers are a common layering pattern for user interaction, we won't really cover controllers in this book; after all, they're a fairly hefty subject on their own and they are two steps removed from the persistence layer, which is the subject of this book.

The Domain Model Layer

The first level in the hierarchy is the domain model. The domain model defines the structure of your information. Your domain model consists of objects that relate to your business. The names of the objects are nouns that are commonly used within your business. In an art gallery application, you'll find domain model objects called `Person`, `Exhibtion`, `Artwork` and `ArtCategory`.

The domain model objects will consist of information that's important to it. For example, a person has a `firstName` and a `lastName`. Domain model objects can also have relationships to other domain model objects. For example, an `Artwork` object may have one or more `ArtCategory` objects that apply to it.

Let's model the `Person` class as follows:

```
public class Person implements Serializable {

    public Integer ADMIN_ROLE_LEVEL = 1;
    public Integer USER_ROLE_LEVEL = 2;
    private Long id;
    private String firstName;
    private String lastName;
    private String username;
    private String password;
    private Integer roleLevel;

    private Integer version;


    public Person() {
```

```
        }
            ...(Getters and setters omitted)
    }
```

The DAO Layer

The goal of the DAO layer is to completely abstract the datasource and ways in which it loads, saves, and manipulates the data at hand. Utilizing the DAO design pattern simplifies code maintenance and enables switching to an alternate persistence framework later. Although switching from a JDBC approach to a Hibernate/ORM approach is fairly rare, a clean design is never a bad thing, and layering your application helps to cleanly separate your code.

There will be DAO layer counterparts to your domain layer objects. For example, in our sample image gallery application, you might create a PersonDAO class to define all the application's persistence needs related to the Person entity. In the PersonDao, you would likely have a method like the following:

```
public Person loadPersonById(Long id);
```

This method would be responsible for loading a Person entity from the database using its unique identifier. Another method might be

```
void savePerson(Person person);
```

This method would be designed to handle all updates to a given row in the Person table (that is, creation or modifications).

When defining a DAO, it is good practice to first write the interface, which delineates all the core persistence-related methods the application will need. We recommend creating separate DAOs for each persistent entity in your domain model, but there are no clear rules in this area. However, defining DAO methods in a separate interface is crucial, as it allows us to write more than one implementation for a give DAO interface. For example, you might have a JDBCPersonDao as well as a

`HibernatePersonDAO`, allowing your application to switch between implementations simply by adjusting the `Spring` configuration.

The Spring Framework also provides a generic data exception hierarchy, suitable for all types of persistence frameworks and usage. Within each persistence framework integration library, Spring does an excellent job of converting each framework-specific exception into an exception that is part of Spring's generic data-access exception hierarchy. Unlike some persistence frameworks, all of the exceptions in Spring's generic exception hierarchy are unchecked, meaning your application code is not required to catch them. But they are accessible should your code need to handle a particular type of exception, and since they are generic, Spring limits your dependency on a particular persistence framework, allowing you to code to a generic and well defined exception hierarchy that can be used for any persistence technology.

The Service Layer

The service layer is intended to accomplish three tasks:

- Serve as the core API through which other layers of your application will interface (this is the incarnation of the facade pattern).

- Define the core business logic, usually calling on one or more DAO methods to achieve this goal.

- Define transactional details for each facade method.

The service layer is the code that defines your application's business logic. In certain cases, some of the methods in this layer may simply be a regurgitation of methods in your DAO layer. More often, methods in the service layer are composed of one or more DAO methods, combined to ensure one or more database operations complete atomically as a single unit of work. For example, in our image gallery application, we might have this method:

```
Person loginUser(String username, String password);
```

The `loginUser()` method is intended to authenticate a user (that is, verify that the specified username and password match) and then load important user information into the session (grab user information, such as name, previous login date, role type, and so on). These tasks would unlikely be handled by a single DAO method. Instead, we would probably combine the `PersonDAO` methods

```
Person authenticateUser(
    String username, String password);
```

with the `RoleDAO` methods:

```
Role getRoleTypeForPersonId(Long userId);
```

Together, these combined DAO methods accomplish a core business goal that is greater than the sum of its parts. In this example, we are using two read-only methods, but imagine a scenario in which we have a business method like so:

```
Boolean transferMoney(
    Long amount,
    Account fromAccount,
    Account destAccount)
    throws InvalidPermissionException,
            NotEnoughFundsException;
```

Now, assume that the preceding service layer method is composed of several DAO methods:

```
Boolean validateSufficientFundsInAccount(
    Long accountId);
Boolean removeFunds(Long accountId, Long amount);
Boolean addFunds(Long accountId, Long amount);
```

It's easy to see what's going on here: we verify that enough cash exists in a particular account and then pull the funds from one account and transfer them to the destination account. The task is easy enough, but it doesn't take an overactive imagination to visualize the hysteria that might ensue should this business method fail halfway through the process: the funds might be withdrawn but never get deposited into the destination account. That might be good for the bank at first, but after a short while, the entire economy collapses, and civilization is left with only a rudimentary barter system where currency degrades to a rudimentary system comprised of crazy straws and *Star Wars* action figures.

Service facade methods typically group together multiple DAO methods to accomplish business logic as a single unit of work. This is the concept of a *transaction*: the entire method and all of its side-effects complete 100 percent successfully, or the application is rolled back to the state before the method was ever called. Before Spring persistence came on the scene, transactional requirements often prompted developers to look toward EJBs, as EJBs would allow developers to declaratively configure transactional semantics for each facade method.

Understanding Your Persistence Options

Throughout the rest of the book, we will illustrate how Spring integrates with several key persistence frameworks and strategies. Along the way, you will learn more about Spring's features and capabilities and some of the key design patterns it uses to get the job done effectively.

When it comes to selecting a persistence framework for your application, there is no wrong answer. Until several years ago, simple JDBC was one of the most popular choices for implementing an application's persistence tier. However, EJB and myriad open source ORM frameworks have significantly changed the persistence landscape, by allowing developers to focus on a Java-based domain model, maintaining the object-oriented semantics of Java without requiring too much thought about the relational world of SQL.

However, things aren't always as easy as they seem: ORM is not without its drawbacks and consequences. First off, there is the issue that has come to be known as the *impedance mismatch* between the object-oriented Java world and the relational SQL world. ORM frameworks, such as Hibernate, do their best to address this mismatch by offering extensive options for mapping between SQL and Java, but fundamental differences between these two worlds will always exist and therefore can't be fully addressed. For instance, concepts such as polymorphism and reference equality have no true analog in the relational database world and therefore must be approximated to the best of the framework's ability.

Despite some of these limitations, ORM frameworks offer numerous benefits by helping to abstract developers from the rigors of a database. For instance, most ORM frameworks introduce ancillary features, such as caching and lazy loading, which can improve the performance of an application dramatically with little or no additional coding effort. ORM frameworks also provide tools to seamlessly generate database schemas and even keep them in sync with the Java-based domain model.

As we cover other persistence frameworks in this book, we'll discuss some of these benefits and drawbacks in more detail. Throughout this book, we will use code samples from an image gallery application that we will be building over the next few chapters. The source code for this application includes implementations that leverage Hibernate, iBATIS, JDBC, Java Content Repository (JCR), Grails, and JPA. We will also be covering Grails and JCR in Chapters 8 and 9. All source code and examples can be downloaded from the Apress web site at www.apress.com.

Summary

This chapter provided you with an overview of Spring, including Inversion of Control (IoC), Aspect Oriented Programming (AOP), and some useful Spring classes. You got an overview on the topic of persistence, including available persistence technologies and transaction management. You also caught a glimpse of application layering best practices, and you got a dose of bad humor. We're going to build on this foundation throughout the book (especially the bad humor).

In the next chapter, we'll start off our image gallery application using good old JDBC. In many circles, JDBC has gotten a pretty bad name, due to the very verbose code and exception catching it often requires. However, you'll soon learn that Spring addresses most of these concerns, often making JDBC integration easier than working with an ORM framework. In fact, we'll even develop our own (very simple) ORM abstraction using Spring JDBC!

Chapter 2: Using Spring JDBC

JDBC was a significant achievement when it first appeared on the scene nearly a decade ago. It provided a clean, clear abstraction for interfacing with any database, staying true to the platform-independence credo of Java. But in practice, JDBC can be quite a difficult beast to tame. Working with a database may seem simple at first, but a lot is happening under the abstraction hood, meaning there's plenty of room for things to go awry. Interacting with a database implicitly means interfacing with a driver, making a connection over a network, and finally initiating SQL calls in which data is passed back and forth between your application and the external database. JDBC does a great job of abstracting this large stack of processes and protocols, but with so much complexity and margin for error, you can easily see how your code might grow commensurately, in order to address all the potential problems and error conditions that might arise.

The complexity surrounding a typical JDBC flow has always been the largest hurdle in working with JDBC: several exceptions must be caught, and steps are required along the way to connect, query, and close a database and its underlying connection. Fortunately, Spring comes to the rescue by providing templates designed to handle the repetitive tedium that represents the vast majority of typical JDBC code. The template design pattern is an ideal solution for these types of scenarios. In the case of Spring JDBC, the template pattern is used to execute the constant, boilerplate steps that are needed for any JDBC operation, such as opening a connection, catching any exceptions (and translating them to Spring's generic exception hierarchy), and ensuring the database connection gets closed. During this sequential process, the template will delegate to your code for the important parts, for instance, the querying for a particular row in the `Person` table that has an `ID` of 3521.

This strategy is used across all of Spring's persistence framework integration points. But the Spring JDBC template is perhaps the most effective at cutting away the code fat to allow you to focus on the purpose at hand: querying and updating your SQL database. This chapter will walk you through the steps needed to get up and running with Spring JDBC. Let's get started!

Integrating JDBC into Your Application Using Spring

In the last chapter, we covered the high-level view of a persistence-based application, illustrating the core layers of a typical Spring application:

- Domain model
- DAO layer
- Service facade layer
- Controller/business logic layer

Most of our efforts in this book will focus on the DAO layer, as this is bulk of your persistence code and configuration. However, the service facade layer is vitally important as well, as this layer is responsible for combining methods defined in your DAOs and assembling them into a cohesive business method that defines an atomic unit of work—at this level, transactional semantics are typically applied. You'll learn later how Spring makes it easy to apply transactional details (that is, how and when data should be committed to the database or rolled back) via configuration, through the application of AOP concepts to your existing code. But before we get ahead of ourselves, let's take a couple steps back and look at the base configuration we will need to get started with our application.

Integrating Datasources with Spring JDBC

JDBC almost always implies a relational database, so starting there makes the most sense. The Java platform has evolved into one for building enterprise-level applications, so the options for connecting to a standard relational database are considerable. At the simplest level, we can instantiate the database driver for our database of choice, but most applications require more than that. Many application servers utilize database connection pools to improve performance when multiple clients are using the application concurrently. To simplify administration and integration, many application servers use JNDI to interface with a database. JNDI is often described as the opposite of Spring's IoC: instead of having dependencies automatically injected into your application, JNDI allows dependencies to be looked up from a centrally managed directory. There are certainly benefits to both approaches. For example, in the case of JNDI, developers can define representative names for database resources but allow an administrator to associate (and change) an actual database with a name at any given time. When a database migration is required, JNDI can simplify some of these administrative tasks, as no changes to the application configuration will be required.

No matter which approach you decide to take, Spring's foundation on interface-based concepts makes integrating a datasource into your application easy. The key factor is that Spring's persistence templates never require a specific type of datasource implementation. Instead, they all depend on the more generic `javax.sql.DataSource` interface. Whether you intend to use a database connection pool or a JNDI-retrieved datasource, the resultant configuration should always produce a standard `javax.sql.Datasource` reference. This brings us to a key concept in Spring: the `Factory-Bean` construct. The `Factory-Bean` is Spring's answer to the well-known factory design pattern, instructing Spring to delegate the instantiation of a bean to the class specified in the configuration. The key concept here is that you are removing a dependency to a specific implementation by delaying the selection or instantiation of the class until runtime. Instead, you define a factory, and it is the factory's job to pick the correct implementation at runtime and instantiate (or look up) that specific class.

The Spring `Factory-Bean` concept is quite similar. Normally in Spring, when you define a bean, the class specified by the `classname` attribute is the class that will be instantiated and injected into other beans that specify that bean as a dependency. This isn't the case with a `Factory-Bean`. When you use a `Factory-Bean`, you are instead instantiating a factory class that will then be responsible for creating the specific implementation used to resolve dependencies in Spring. So essentially, the `classname` attribute in this case just defines a factory implementation, whose job will then be to create the actual target implementation you need.

It's easy to understand now how this concept will allow us to employ multiple strategies to access a datasource without tying ourselves down to a particular solution. If you use the `JndiObjectFactoryBean` (a factory bean for resolving JNDI datasources), you will still end up with a `DataSource` reference, and the same will occur if you choose to use the `PooledDatasource` implementation. There are other reasons to use a `Factory-Bean` in Spring, as well. For instance, a `MapFactoryBean` can be utilized to create a Java `Map`, entirely in your configuration file (which can be quite convenient in certain cases).

Spring `Factory-Beans` implement the `FactoryBean` interface, which defines three methods designed to instantiate the target object (that is, the instance the factory is intended to create), specify the target object's type, and indicate whether the target object is a singleton or prototype. For our scenario, we would configure our JNDI datasource in the following way:

```
<bean id="datasource" class=
  "org.springframework.jndi.JndiObjectFactoryBean">
  <property name="jndiName"
    value="java:comp/env/jdbc/GalleryDS"/>
</bean>
```

This configuration can be made even simpler using Spring's support for namespaces. Namespace support was introduced in Spring 2.0 and helps to simplify configuration. Although the preceding example is fairly concise, in some situations, configuration can be made more easily readable and terse by importing a namespace intended to handle a specific type of configuration. For example, by importing the `jndi` namespace, we can simplify the preceding JNDI lookup further:

```
<jee:jndi-lookup id="datasource"
    jndi-name="java:comp/env/jdbc/GalleryDS"/>
```

Not only have we reduced the configuration to a single line, the intention of our configuration is now even clearer. We'll discuss some of the benefits and implications of utilizing Spring's namespace support later in this chapter.

Although we have examined various details of Spring configuration, we have not yet explained how these disparate pieces fit together. How does your Spring configuration file get loaded? Where does it go? Where do we start? Where do babies come from? Unfortunately, none of these questions have a simple answer. This is actually a good thing: Spring is quite flexible, and the approach you take for integrating Spring into your application will depend on the type of application you are building.

Creating an ApplicationContext

The important concept to understand is that Spring's job is to parse your configuration files and then instantiate your managed classes, resolving their interdependencies. Spring is often called a container, since it is designed to create and manage all the dependencies within your application, serving as a foundation and context through which beans may also be looked up. This core engine is represented by a base interface called `BeanFactory`. The `BeanFactory` defines the core Spring engine that conglomerates your beans and wires the collaborating dependencies together. But the Spring container is capable of much more than just dependency injection. The Spring container may also be used to publish events, provide AOP functionality, support a resource loading abstraction, facilitate internationalization, and so on. For many of these advanced capabilities, you will need to use an `ApplicationContext` implementation.

The `ApplicationContext` extends the `BeanFactory` interface, providing a set of more robust features. The separation can come in handy if you are building a very lightweight application and don't need some of these more advanced features. But for most applications (especially server-side software), you will want to use an `ApplicationContext` implementation. In the case of web applications, you will typically use a `WebApplicationContext`. Spring ships with a `listener` that you can throw into your `web.xml` file to automatically bootstrap the Spring `ApplicationContext` and load up your configuration file. It's as easy as adding the following lines into your `web.xml`:

```
<listener>
   <listener-class>org.springframework.web. ➥
context.request.RequestContextListener
</listener-class>
</listener>
```

These lines will ensure that Spring gets loaded when your application first starts up and will parse the configuration file located at `WEB-INF/applicationcontext.xml`.

If you're not building a web application, it's just as easy to bootstrap the Spring container. We recommend going with the `ClassPathXmlApplicationContext` implementation, which is designed to load the Spring configuration files from the classpath. It is invoked in the following way:

```
ApplicationContext context =
   new ClassPathXmlApplicationContext( new String[]
     {"configfile1.xml", "configfile2.xml"});
```

You can see just how easy it is to get a Spring container instantiated. Once you have a reference to the `ApplicationContext`, you can use it however you wish. The reference that is returned to you is the loaded `ApplicationContext`, with all the beans that you defined instantiated and dependencies resolved. If you felt so inclined, you could access a bean by name, simply by invoking this:

```
UsefulClass usefulClass =
   (UsefulClass) context.getBean("myBeanName");
```

Assuming that your bean is defined somewhere in your Spring configuration files (referenced by the `id` or `name` attribute), Spring will hand you your class instance, ready to go (meaning all of its dependencies will have been injected). However, we strongly recommend that you try to avoid issuing calls to `getBean()`. The whole point of Spring is automatic dependency injection, which means not looking up your beans when you need them (that's dependency lookup, which is so 1995). As a rule of thumb, if you need a reference to a particular dependency, specify these details in the configuration, not in your code. Some developers will rely on `getBean()` only in circumstances in which they *always* need a new instance of their class (each time they make the call). You'll learn later a better solution to this problem using `lookup-method`, which coerces Spring to override or implement the specified method with code that will always return a new instance of a designated bean.

Using Singleton Beans

By default, beans defined in Spring are all scoped as singletons. A singleton is a class that is guaranteed to only have a single instance in the JVM. Singletons are great for storing application state or any requirement in which you want to be assured that there is only ever one reference in your application. Normally, you would need to write code to achieve this assurance. The typical singleton meets the following criteria:

- Has a static method to return the single instance of the class (stored as a static reference within the class)

- Has a private constructor, ensuring that only the singleton itself can ever create a new instance (which is your assurance that you won't accidentally create more than once instance, simply by invoking new `MySingleton()`)

So, a singleton in your application might resemble the following:

```
class MySingleton {
  private static MySingleton instance;
  private MySingleton() {
  }

  public static MySingleton getInstance() {
      return instance;
  }
}
```

Although the preceding sample illustrates a useful design pattern, Spring obviates the need to write this boilerplate code, once again allowing you to move these details into the configuration. Again, by default, all Spring beans are singletons. If this is not your intention, you need to specify a different scope for your bean.

Scopes are a powerful new feature, introduced in Spring 2.0. In Spring 1, beans were either prototype or singleton beans. Prototype means that each new call to `getBean()` would return a brand new instance of your bean. Singleton beans guarantee that there can only ever be a single instance of your class in the entire Spring `ApplicationContext`. Spring 2 offers several powerful new scopes, including `request` and `session` (which ties a bean's life cycle to an active servlet request or session, respectively), as well as the ability to roll your own.

Integrating a Database

Now that you have a clearer picture of how Spring is bootstrapped within your application, let's get back to integrating our database of choice. We've learned that Spring's adherence to interface-based concepts helps to separate implementation choices out of our code and into configuration. So, whether you choose to use a JNDI factory-bean to pull in a database reference from an external JNDI directory or configure a specific database driver directly, your code won't be affected one bit. In the end, we'll always end up with a JDBC DataSource, and that's all your code needs to care about.

In our example, we'll keep things simple. Let's start off by creating a Spring bean that will create a JDBC DataSource instance:

```
<bean id="myDatasource"
class="org.springframework.jdbc.  ↦
datasource.DriverManagerDataSource">
  <property name="url"
    value="jdbc:hsqldb://127.0.0.1/imagegallery"/>
  <property name="driverClassName"
    value="org.hsqldb.jdbcDriver"/>
  <property name="username" value="blah"/>
  <property name="password" value="1234"/>
</bean>
```

Pretty simple, huh? Now, if we wanted to get a bit fancier, we could instead choose a popular database connection pool as our bean implementation. A connection pool is ideal for web applications in which multiple, concurrent database operations will be made. A connection pool can be optimized for different usage scenarios, ensuring a more efficient means for handing off new database connections to the application. Again, switching to a database connection pool will give our application more efficiency without requiring any code changes.

You'll also notice that we have specified a `url` property for our `myDatasource` bean. This property determines the URL at which the application may connect to our database. Different databases will require different JDBC URLs. In this example, we have decided to use the popular HSQL database. HSQL is a Java-based database and is therefore easy to integrate into any Java-based application (it doesn't require an external database process). However, you can just as easily use PostgreSQL, MySQL, or any database for which a JDBC driver is available. Just make sure your database is up, running, and configured to listen on the URL specified in the bean's configuration. It is also critical that you include the appropriate JDBC driver on your classpath when the application is first started. Because HSQL is Java-based, simply including the HSQL JAR file on your classpath is all that is required to get rolling. When it comes time to make your application production ready, you may want to consider a more robust solution, such as PostgreSQL or Oracle.

Adding Persistence

Now we have an application that has a database integrated into it. The next step is to start building our persistence functionality. This is where the DAO layer we described earlier comes into play. The goal of the DAO layer is to encapsulate all database read and write operations required by the application. Typically, you will want to first define an interface that delineates all database operations for a particular domain type. For example, thinking back to our image gallery example, we will need to define a few main domain types (to start):

- `ArtEntity`
- `Exhibition`
- `Person`

The `ArtEntity` class will encapsulate everything about a particular `Image`, such as size information, as well as the location of the image file itself (we could also elect to store the image data in the database).

The `Exhibition` class will relate a group of images together into a collection. So, within our gallery application, we will have many exhibits available for an end user to view, and each `Exhibition` will contain at least one `ArtEntity`. The business goal of the `Exhibition` is to organize a group of `ArtEntity` objects together, according to a particular theme, time period, artist, and so on. The `Exhibit` class may also contain information related to the name of the `Exhibition`, as well as the date range through which the `Exhibit` might be available.

In a well-structured application, we would want to define two separate DAO interfaces: one for the `Exhibit` class and one for the `ArtEntity` class. Next, we define an implementation of each DAO interface. Of course, it is possible to write more than one implementation of each DAO interface, and throughout the course of this book, that is exactly what we plan to do! Each implementation will illustrate a different persistence approach. However, we will begin with Spring JDBC.

Using the Template Pattern for Persistence

When it comes to persistence, Spring utilizes a very consistent approach no matter which persistence framework you elect to use. In each case, Spring makes good use of the template pattern to simplify the code (and effort) required to perform a read or write operation. The template pattern does exactly as its name implies: it extracts boilerplate and redundant tasks into a template, delegating to your specific implementation for functionality that can't be templated. In most cases, the untemplateable code is your persistence logic itself. Using the template pattern means you can just focus on the database operations, without having to worry about the mindless details, such as these boilerplate steps:

- Opening a database connection
- Beginning a transaction
- Wrapping your SQL operations in `try`/`catch` blocks
- Committing or rolling back a transaction
- Closing the database connection
- Catching any exceptions that might occur in transactions or closing the database connection

It's amazing how painfully verbose working with JDBC can be. Without using Spring JDBC, most of your code has little to do with your persistence logic but is the same boilerplate code required by each and every operation.

Spring provides templates for many persistence frameworks, and we will cover some of these in Chapters 3, 4, 5, and 8 (when we discuss Hibernate, JPA, iBATIS, and JCR). For now, we will begin with the `SpringJDBCTemplate` to explain how Spring automates much of the workflow required by JDBC operations.

Working with the Spring JDBCTemplate

The Spring `JDBCTemplate` handles most of the boilerplate operations required by JDBC, delegating to your code for the important parts. It also catches any exceptions that may occur and replaces them with Spring's own data-access exceptions. This conversion allows you to work with a consistent exception hierarchy that is not tied to a specific persistence framework, so you can easily switch between disparate persistence frameworks without having to change the exception handling throughout your code. As mentioned earlier, Spring's exception hierarchy does not use checked exceptions, meaning you aren't required to catch any of these exceptions. When it comes to database operations, unchecked exceptions are far more pragmatic: if something goes awry when you are trying to write to the database, chances are there's nothing your application can do to recover. So what is the point of handling this exception if you can't do much about it anyway?

Let's begin by defining our `PersonDao` interface:

```
public interface PersonDao {

  public Person getPerson(Long personId) ;
  public void savePerson(Person person) ;
  public List<Person> getPeople() ;
  public Person getPersonByUsername(String username) ↪
    throws EntityNotFoundException ;

  public Person authenticatePerson(
    String username, String password)
    throws AuthenticationException;
}
```

With our interface defined, let's begin building our JDBC-based implementation. Since our DAO needs a reference to a datasource, we will define the appropriate setter method, through which Spring will inject our datasource. Our `PersonDao` implementation will begin as follows:

```
public class JdbcPersonDao
  implements PersonDao {
  private JdbcTemplate jdbcTemplate;

  public void setDataSource(DataSource dataSource) {
    this.jdbcTemplate = new JdbcTemplate(dataSource);
  }
}
```

The preceding snippet defines the scaffolding of the JDBC implementation for our `PersonDao` interface. Once the datasource reference is injected (via setter injection), we instantiate a `JdbcTemplate` instance and assign it to our private `jdbcTemplate` member variable. We configure this class in Spring using the following XML:

```
<bean id="personDao"
class="com.dialm4mercury.gallery.dao.JdbcPersonDao">
  <property name="datasource" ref="myDatasource"/>
</bean>
```

Notice that we are passing in the myDatasource bean that we configured earlier in this chapter. Now, when Spring creates our imageGalleryDao bean and passes in a reference to our datasource, the jdbcTemplate will be automatically created. This means that any of our DAO methods will be able to count on jdbcTemplate being configured. However, since our application will only have a single DataSource implementation, we can simplify our configuration by using annotations:

```
@Repository("personDao")
public class JdbcPersonDao
    implements PersonDao {
    private JdbcTemplate jdbcTemplate;

    @Autowired
    public void setDataSource(DataSource dataSource) {
        this.jdbcTemplate = new JdbcTemplate(dataSource);
    }
}
```

The choice over which configuration approach to use largely depends on your coding style. In the preceding example, we use the @Repository annotation, indicating that we are configuring a class with persistence-related functionality. This will allow us to define a component scanner in our Spring configuration, through which Spring will search the appropriate package structure in order to find those classes that match the configured annotation type. To ensure that our PersonDao class will be configured into our Spring ApplicationContext, we will need to add a component-scanning bean like the following to our Spring XML configuration:

```
<context:component-scan base-package=
    "com.smartpants.artwork.dao.jdbc">
  <context:include-filter type="annotation" expression=
      "org.springframework.stereotype.Repository"/>
</context:component-scan>
```

This XML snippet tells Spring to look for classes annotated with
@Repository within the com.smartpants.artwork.dao.jdbc package.
It is also important to point out that we have added the @Autowired
annotation above our setDataSource() setter, requesting that Spring
inject a class of type DataSource into our JdbcPersonDao
implementation.

With configuration out of the way, let's begin implementing our DAO.
First off, we should establish the DAO contract. The PersonDao interface
will be defined as the following:

```
public interface PersonDao {

  public Person getPerson(Long personId) ;
  public void savePerson(Person person) ;
  public List<Person> getPeople() ;
  public Person getPersonByUsername(String username)
    throws EntityNotFoundException ;

  public Person authenticatePerson(
    String username, String password)
      throws AuthenticationException;

}
```

The preceding interface defines the contact for our PersonDao. Regardless
of whichever persistence framework we might choose, this interface serves
as an abstraction of persistence functionality related to the Person domain
entity. Classes that utilize the PersonDao will not need to know or care
about which technology we are using to actually save or load the data.

We've already begun defining our JDBC-based `PersonDao` implementation by allowing a `datasource` to be injected via Spring, as well as instantiating a `jdbcTempate` for use with all of our DAO methods. Now, let's get down to the persistence logic itself.

Using RowMapper

One of the most common persistence-related tasks is defining a DAO method that finds an entity by its primary key (or ID). An object's natural identifier (as well as its corresponding record in the database) is inherently unique, so as a consequence, we can always expect a single object when we retrieve an object by its ID. However, we need to figure out an effective way to map from the column-based world of the relational database to the object-oriented world of Java. Luckily, Spring provides an easy solution in the form of the `RowMapper`. A `RowMapper` is a simple interface that takes as parameters a `ResultSet` (the returned result set from the database) and an `int` (representing a row number) and returns an `Object`. The `Object` that is returned is the domain object that your `RowMapper` implementation will create. For example, a `RowMapper` for our purposes might look like the following:

```
RowMapper personMappergalleryMapper = new RowMapper() {
  public Object mapRow(ResultSet rs, int rowNum)
      throws SQLException {
    Person person = new Person();
    person.setId(rs.getLong("id"));
    person.setFirstname(rs.getString("first_name"));
    person.setLastname(rs.getString("last_name"));
    person.setUsername(rs.getString("user_name"));

    return person;
  }
};
```

The `ResultSet` passed into the `mapRow` method is the `ResultSet` returned by the SQL query we must define. In our implementation, we create a new instance of our `Gallery` domain object and then pull the data we need out of the `ResultSet` so that it can be applied to our new `Person` instance. For instance, the code `rs.getString("first_name")` attempts to pull the data in the column `gallery_name` out of the current row in the `ResultSet`. This ends up serving as a really effective way to convert the data returned from the database into our object-oriented domain model. In the next chapter, you'll learn how an ORM framework such as Hibernate can take care of this translation automatically. But in cases where we have fairly simple domain models (or even very complex ones), writing the code required to handle this translation ourselves is often easier.

Implementing Our DAO Interface

Now that we've defined a `RowMapper` for converting a SQL `ResultSet` into a `Gallery` object, let's see how we can integrate this code into our DAO implementation.

First off, we need to define our SQL queries. In our interface, we have one query that returns a single `Person` object (querying by its ID) and another query that returns a collection of `Person` objects. Additionally, we have a conditional method that finds a `Person` entitiy that matches a specific username. Since the conversion between a `ResultSet` and a `Person` object will always be the same, whether we return a single instance or a thousand, we can utilize the same `RowMapper` implementation for the `getPersonById` method as for the `getPersonByUsername` and `getPeople` methods. Therefore, it makes sense to abstract the `RowMapper` code into a static innerclass:

```
private static final class PersonMapperGalleryMapper
    implements RowMapper {
  RowMapper galleryMapper = new RowMapper() {
    public Object mapRow(ResultSet rs, int rowNum)
      throws SQLException {
      Person person = new Person();
      person.setId(rs.getLong("id"));
      person.setFirstname(rs.getString("first_name"));
      person.setLastname(rs.getString("last_name"));
      person.setUsername(rs.getString("user_name"));

      return person;
    }
  };
}
```

Now, we can easily reference this `RowMapper` implementation for either
method, simply by instantiating it:

```
private static final String getPersonByIdSql =
    "select first_name, last_name, id " +
    "from Person where id = ?";
public Person getPersonById(Long id) {
  Person person = (Person) this.jdbcTemplate
    .queryForObject(getPersonByIdSql,
      new Object[] {id}, new PersonMapper());
  return person;
}
```

Notice we first define our SQL query, storing it into a `private static`
constant. We could also choose to abstract our SQL into our Spring
configuration files and inject the queries via standard setter injection. This
approach would allow us to easily modify queries without having to
recompile our code. Additionally, it would ensure that all of our SQL was
stored in a centralized location, making maintenance easier. For instance,
we might append our Spring configuration in the following way:

```
<bean id="personDao"
class=""="com.dialm4mercury.gallery.dao.JdbcPersonDao">
  <property name="datasource" ref="myDatasource"/>
  <property name="personByIdSql">
    <value>
      select first_name, last_name, id
      from Person where id = ?
    </value>
  </property>
</bean>
```

Then, within our JdbcPersonDao implementation, we would define a
property and corresponding setter method, through which Spring will inject
our SQL query template:

```
public class JdbcPersonDao
  implements PersonDao {
  private JdbcTemplate jdbcTemplate;

  private personByIdSql;
  public void setPersonByIdSql(String sql) {
    this.personByIdSql = sql;
  }
  public String getPersonByIdSql() {
    return this.personByIdSql;
  }

  public void setDataSource(DataSource dataSource) {
    this.jdbcTemplate = new JdbcTemplate(dataSource);
  }

}
```

The important part of the code is our implementation of the
getPersonById method. In our getPersonById(Long id)
implementation, we reference the JdbcTemplate, calling the
queryForObject method. JdbcTemplate supports a range of query
methods, the most common of which is queryForObject. However, it is

also common to use `JdbcTemplate` to perform more trivial SQL queries that have simpler return types, such as an `int` or `String`. Because these types of methods only return a simple, scalar value, no complex mapping is needed.

For example, you could write code that returned the number of `Person` entities stored in the database using the following method:

```
public int getNumGalleries() {
  return this.jdbcTemplate.queryForInt(
    "select count(*) from Person");
}
```

Or we could write a projection query, in which we are just extracting a single field from our `Person` entity:

```
public String getUsernameById(Long id) {
  return this.jdbcTemplate.queryForString(
    "select user_name from Person where id = ?",
    new Object[] {id});
}
```

However, we don't need either of these methods in our `PersonDao`; we just thought it would be important to demonstrate other ways in which the `JdbcTemplate` could be used for more simple SQL operations.

Let's now write the implementation to load all `Person` entities:

```
private static final String peopleSql =
  "select first_name, last_name, user_name, id " +
  "from Person";
public List<Person> getPeople() {
  Collection<Person> people =
    this.jdbcTemplate.query(
      peopleSql,
      new Object[] {date},
      new PersonMapper());
  return new ArrayList<Person>(people);
}
```

Notice that we use the same `PersonMapper`, but we now call the `JdbcTemplate` query method instead of `queryForObject`. The query method returns a `Collection`, but since our interface specifies that this method returns a list, we create an empty list and add all of the returned collection elements to this list. However, the method works in much the same way as the previous query method—even sharing the same `PersonMapper`.

For our last `PersonDao` interface method, we don't need to perform any SQL queries. Instead, we need to insert a record into the database, corresponding to a new `Person` instance. Spring provides several flexible options for handling database write operations, including inserts, updates, and even DDL operations. The simplest way to insert new rows into the database is via the `SimpleJdbc` classes. These abstractions provide an intuitive means for writing to the database, using database metadata to simplify configuration. Spring makes this type of operation even easier than the previous query examples. It is also possible to use the `JdbcTemplate`'s update methods to handle update and insert operations, but the `SimpleJdbc` classes really come in handy to simplify database writes.

Using the SimpleJdbc Classes

Although it's usually ideal to specify the SQL you wish to execute explicitly, Spring provides a simplified means for inserting data or calling stored procedures using the `SimpleJdbcInsert` and `SimpleJdbcCall` classes respectively. The `SimpleJdbc` approach utilizes database metadata to infer details about the table structure into which you intend to insert data, reducing much of the configuration required to achieve your end goal.

The best approach for using `SimpleJdbc` is to instantiate an instance of the `SimpleJdbc` class for each database operation you wish to initiate. Using our `PersonDao` example, the most ideal location for initialization is within the `setDataSource(Datasource dataSource)` method (into which Spring will inject our `DataSource` reference):

```
public class JdbcPersonDao implements PersonDao {
  private JdbcTemplate jdbcTemplate;
  private personByIdSql;

  private SimpleJdbcInsert insertPerson;

  public void setDataSource(DataSource dataSource) {
    this.jdbcTemplate = new JdbcTemplate(dataSource);
    this.insertPerson = new SimpleJdbcInsert(dataSource)
      .withTableName("person")
      .usingGeneratedKeyColumns("id");
  }
```

The preceeding code will instantiate our `insertPerson` member variable to be used for inserting new rows into the `Person` database. Notice that `SimpleJdbcInsert` uses method chaining, allowing multiple methods to be called sequentially on the same line. The `withTable` method must be passed the precise name of the table on which you plan to operate, as this is how metadata will be extracted (for instance, inferring the column names used within the table). The `usingGeneratedKeyColumns` method is optional, but it allows the `SimpleJdbc` class to rely on the database for generating a primary key for the newly inserted row. It is important to ensure that you are using a driver that supports autogenerated keys in order for this feature to work properly. Optionally, you can omit this method and instead pass the `id` for the new row explicitly. Let's now look at how new data is inserted.

Once our `insertPerson` member variable is initialized, we can use it for creating new rows in our `Person` table. Let's define an alternative `savePerson(Person person)` method, using the `SimpleJdbcInsert` strategy:

```
private static final String savePersonSql =
  "insert into Person(first_name, last_name, ↩
  first_name, username, id) values (?,?,?,?,?)";

public void savePerson(Person person) {
  Map<String, Object> parameters = ↩
      new HashMap<String, Object>(2);
  parameters.put("first_name", person.getFirstName());
  parameters.put("last_name", person.getLastName());
  parameters.put("username", person.getUserName());
  Number generatedId = insertPerson.executeAndReturnKey(
    parameters);
  person.setId(generatedId.longValue());
}
```

In the preceding method, we define a new `HashMap` and put the corrpesponding column names and values from our `Person` instance. Once we've configured our `HashMap`, we then call `executeAndReturnKey()` on our `insertPerson` member variable, passing in the `Map` we've just configured. Notice that the `executeAndReturnKey()` method returns a `Number`. This is the autogenerated primary key for our newly inserted row. We then set the `id` property on our `Person` reference, so that our `Person` instance has a reference back to its corresponding row in the database.

If we chose not to use the autogenerated key approach (by omitting the `usingGeneratedColumns()` call when configuring our `SimpleJdbcInsert` reference), we could generate the preceding ourselves using the alternative approach:

```
Public void savePerson(Person person) {
  Map<String, Object> parameters =
    new HashMap<String, Object>(2);
  parameters.put("first_name", person.getFirstName());
  parameters.put("last_name", person.getLastName());
```

```
   parameters.put("username", person.getUserName());
   parameters.put("id"), person.getId());
   insertPerson.execute(parameters);
}
```

In the example preceding, we configure our preceding directly, by setting it in the parameters `HashMap`. Additionally, we now call the `execute` method, which does not return anything (since we already know the primary key for this row).

The preceding examples could be simplified even further if our column names exactly matched the property names in our `Person` class (or within an optional `Person` DTO class). In this scenario, we could use the following line instead of configuring each column name and value within a `HashMap`:

```
SqlParameterSource parameters =
   New BeanPropertySqlParameterSource(person);
```

The `SqlParameterSource` class will use the properties from the passed in `Person` reference for configuring the database insert.

Updating and Executing via JdbcTemplate

Although the `SimpleJdbc` classes can reduce your code significantly, they aren't ideal for all scenarios. For instance, if we would like to define a method for updating a row in our `Person` table, we can create the following method:

```
private static final String updatePersonSql =
   "update Person set first_name = ?, " +
   "last_name = ?, username = ? " +
   "where id = ?";

public void updatePerson(Person person) {
   this.jdbcTemplate.update(
     updatePersonSql,
     new Object[]{
```

```
        person.getFirstname(),
        person.getLastname(),
        person.getUsername(),
        person.getId()}); 
}
```

The preceding method will extract the fields from the `Person` reference and use this data to construct an update statement. This all seems rather trivial, but keep in mind that Spring is taking care of a lot of details under the hood, including handling exceptions and translating them into Spring's `DataAccess` exception hierarchy.

Handling Binary Data

Our `PersonDao` is fairly straightforward, as it only needs to manipulate simple `String` fields. However, since we are building a gallery application, we will eventually need to handle more complex data types. We could choose to store image data on the filesystem, instead only storing path references to the location in which images are stored. However, we've found that it is often more flexible to put everything in the database, ensuring your application data is completely centralized (and portable).

In the database world, binary large objects (BLOBs) are used to represent large binary fields, while character large objects (CLOBs) are used to represent large amounts of character data. The process for working with these field types in Spring is largely the same. First, we need to create a `DefaultLobHandler` reference to be used within our inserts and queries; this Spring abstraction is intended to simplify the manipulation of BLOB and CLOB fields. We can create our `DefaultLobHander` by adding the following snippet to our Spring configuration:

```
<bean id="defaultLobHandler" class=
   "org.springframework.jdbc.support. ↪
lob.DefaultLobHandler" />
```

Next, we need to inject our `defaultLobHandler` reference into our DAO layer. We don't need BLOB support in our `PersonDao` implementation, and we haven't gotten to our `ArtEntityDao` just yet (we will in subsequent chapters). To conserve space, we won't get into the details of our `ArtEntityDao` here. Just keep in mind that this interface will handle persistence operations for the `ArtEntity` domain object (which represents a particular image within our gallery application).

Let's begin stubbing out our `JdbcArtEntityDao` implementation:

```
public class JdbcArtEntityDao implements ArtEntityDao {
    private JdbcTemplate jdbcTemplate;
    private LobHandler defaultLobHandler;
    // getters and setters omitted
}
```

We will, of course, need to ensure our `lobHandler` reference is injected into our `JdbcArtEntityDao` class. Next, let's define a `saveArtEntity` method that takes an `ArtEntity` reference, which encapsuates information about our image as well as the image data itself. Again, keep in mind that this is a simplification of our actual `ArtEntityDao` interface and domain entity; both will be defined in more detail later in this book. Our `saveArtEntity` method might look like the following:

```
public void saveArtEntity(ArtEntity artEntity) {
    int numRowsAffeted = jdbcTemplate.update(
      "INSERT INTO ARTENTITY " +
      "(name, title, subtitle, description, imageData)" +
      "VALUES (?, ?, ?, ?, ?)",
      new Object[] {
        artEntity.getName(),
        artEntity.getTitle(),
        artEntity.getSubTitle(),
        artEntity.getDescription(),
        new SqlLobValue(
          artEntity.getImageData(),
          defaultLobHandler)
```

```
    },
    new int[] {
      Types.VARCHAR,
      Types.VARCHAR,
      Types.VARCHAR,
      Types.VARCHAR,
      Types.BLOB });
```

```
}
```

Notice that we are instantiating a new instance of the `SqlLobValue` class, passing in the `byte array` pulled from our `ArtEntity` instance along with our `defaultLobHandler` reference. We then add this `SqlLobValue` instance to our `Object` array of SQL parameter values. Once the `update` method is invoked, it returns the number of rows affected by the operation. In this case, our new single row should be added to the database, and our variable `numRowsAffected` should be equal to the value of 1.

Working with BLOBs and CLOBs during query operations is very similar to the examples illustrated previously. For instance, we might have a method in our `JdbcArtEntityDao` implementation called `ArtEntity getArtEntityById(Long id)`. As in our previous examples, we would first define a `RowMapper` for our `ArtEntity` domain object:

```
public static final class ArtEntityMapper
    implements RowMapper {

  public Object mapRow(ResultSet rs, int i)
      throws SQLException {
    ArtEntity artEntity = new ArtEntity();
    byte[] imageData= defaultLobHandler
      .getBlobAsBytes(rs, 4);
    String description = rs.getString("description");
    String title = rs.getString("title");
    String subtitle = rs.getString("subTitle")
    String name = rs.getString("name");
    artEntity.setName(name);
```

```
    artEntity.setDescription(description);
    artEntity.setTitle(title);
    artEntity.setSubTitle(subtitle);
    artEntity.setImageData(imageData);
    return artEntity;
  }
}
```

With our `RowMapper` defined, we can now use it within any of the query methods described previously. Notice that we utilized our `defaultLobHandler` to help extract binary data from the `ResultSet`.

```
this.jdbcTemplate.update(
  savePersonSql,
  new Object[]{
    person.getFirstname(),
    person.getLastname(),
    person.getUsername(),
    person.getId()});
}
```

The preceding method will extract the fields from the `Person` reference and use this data to construct an insert statement. This all seems quite simple, but keep in mind that Spring is taking care of a lot of details under the hood. If you attempted to perform these same SQL operations in plain JDBC, you would have to write at least ten times the code. Using Spring JDBC, you can instead focus on the business logic and the aspects that are unique to your application.

Other JdbcTemplate Implementatons

Now that we've defined our `PersonDao`, we can move on to other parts of our gallery application. In the next chapters, we will continue to build on the functionality we have already defined. However, there is still a bit more to learn about Spring JDBC. Staying true to Spring's motto of flexibility, there are several other `JdbcTemplate` implementations, each designed to work in a slightly different manner. For example, the NamedParameterJdbcTemplate allows you to specify your SQL parameters more explicitly, which makes for cleaner code and leaves less room for error (since there will be no confusion over which SQL parameter is intended for each parameter).

Another JdbcTemplate derivative is the SimpleJdbcTemplate. This implementation is designed to better utilize Java 5 features, such as generics. For example, in our first query method, we were required to cast the Object returned by our RowMapper implementation to the Person domain object. Using the SimpleJdbcTemplate, we could have instead written our RowMapper in the following way:

```
private static final class PersonMapper
    implements ParameterizedRowMapper<Person> {
  ParameterizedRowMapper<Person> personMapper =
    new ParameterizedRowMapper<Person>() {
      public Person mapRow(ResultSet rs, int rowNum)
        throws SQLException {
        Person person = new Person();
        person.setId(rs.getLong("id"));
        person.setFirstName(rs.getString("first_name"));
        person.setLastName(rs.getString("last_name"));
        person.setUsername(rs.getString("user_name"));
        return person;
      }
    };
  return personMapper;
}
```

Now, our PersonMapper returns a Person domain object instead of a simple Object. The difference is subtle, but it leads to much cleaner code. However, the ParameterizedRowMapper can only be used with the SimpleJdbcTemplate and requires Java 5.

Summary

In this chapter, we covered some of the basics of bootstrapping a Spring `ApplicationContext`, as well as integrating a `DataSource` into our application. We've also started to build the DAO layer for our gallery application using Spring JDBC.

In the next chapter, we'll continue building our sample application, but we'll switch over to Hibernate. You will start to notice how Spring applies the same general design patterns for each persistence framework. However, Hibernate brings along some other interesting benefits, such as lazy loading and caching.

Chapter 3: Using Spring with Hibernate

Much like Spring, Hibernate changed the software development landscape when it first appeared on the scene. The timing was ideal: developers were frustrated by other ORM frameworks such as EJB. Hibernate attempted to solve the persistence problem through simplicity and clean, thoughtful design.

Also like Spring, Hibernate relies heavily on the JavaBean concept, which accounts for a significant aspect of its success. Other ORM frameworks force developers to muddy their domain models with restrictive and rigid requirements, such as alternate and parent classes, as well as Data Transfer Objects (DTOs). Hibernate enables persistence with little reliance or coupling to Hibernate. Spring helps to decouple Hibernate further through the use of `HibernateDaoSupport` and `HibernateTemplate` classes, which serve to simplify and standardize integration and persistence operations.

Looking back, it is easy to see how Spring and Hibernate were instrumental to each other's success. With philosophies that stressed lightweight methodologies, simplicity, and code cleanliness, the Hibernate-Spring duo ushered in a new age for Java persistence. This mutual success had a dramatic impact on the Java community and was the catalyst for numerous changes that embraced a lighter-weight approach to application development and persistence.

Migrating Our Gallery Application to Hibernate

This chapter will continue to build on our sample gallery application utilizing Spring and now Hibernate. In our previous chapter, we discussed some of the core infrastructural components required by an application's persistence tier.

Part of the beauty of Spring is the way in which it transparently decouples the components of your application, so swapping our JDBC DAO implementation with a Hibernate solution is reasonably trivial. Spring also provides a consistent exception hierarchy, meaning there is very little coupling to any persistence framework in our code. If we need to work with both Spring JDBC and Hibernate together within the same application, this decoupling makes things much easier.

Hibernate's strength is the ease with which developers can begin building a persistence tier. The first step is usually to define your domain model using simple JavaBeans (or POJOs). In the last chapter, we introduced several core classes that comprise the root of our application's domain model. In this chapter, we will build on this foundation, introducing a few additional classes.

Defining the Associations

Earlier, we discussed the `ArtEntity` class that will represent artwork, images, and photos in our gallery application. Our domain model will also include a `Comment` class that will be used to represent an individual comment about a particular `ArtEntity`. An `ArtEntity` will naturally contain multiple comments to allow for an unlimited number of site visitors to add their own comments about the particular piece of art they are viewing. Although an `ArtEntity` may contain multiple `Comment` instances, a given `Comment` can only reference a single `ArtEntity`, as typically a comment is intended to relate to a particular piece of content within the gallery application. The association between an `ArtEntity` and its `Comment` instances is best described as one-to-many relationship. Inversely, the relationship between a `Comment` and its associated `ArtEntity` is known as a many-to-one association.

It's always important to consider the way in which the domain model and its relationships will be translated into a database schema, even when ORM abstractions often handle these details for us. This example association will require two tables: an `Art_Entity` table and a `Comment` table. An `ArtEntity` instance will then be associated with a `Comment` through a foreign key reference to the `Art_Entity` in the `Comment` table; see Figure 3-1.

Figure 3-1. The relationship between the Art_Entity and Comment tables

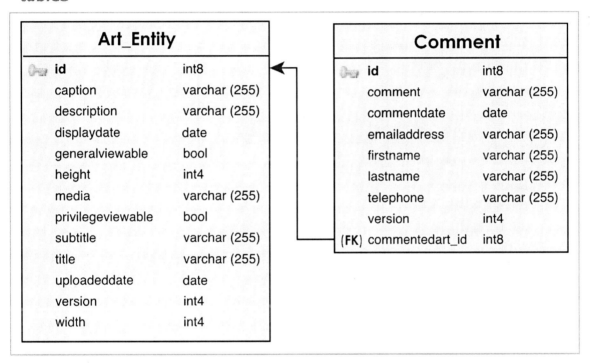

Our gallery application will also require a `Category` class used to represent a category into which a particular `ArtEntity` may be placed (to help organize artwork and photos into logical groups). Each `Category` may contain more than one `ArtEntity`. Similarly, each `ArtEntity` may be placed into multiple `Category` instances. This type of association is normally referred to as many-to-many. The many-to-many association is a bit more complicated than one-to-many. The best way to model this type of relationship in the database is to utilize a join table. A join table simply contains foreign keys from the two related tables, allowing a row from each table to be associated with each other. The following diagram in Figure 3-2 will help illustrate the relationship between an `Art_Entity` and a `Category`:

Figure 3-2. Relationship between ArtEntity and Category

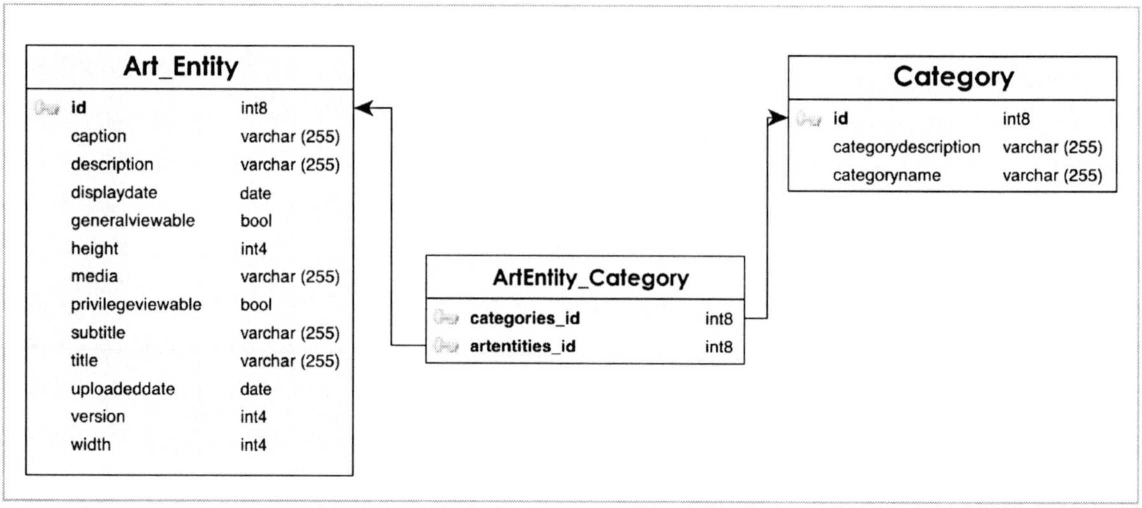

Although it is important to have a clear understanding of your domain model's table structure, Hibernate can take care of creating these database-specific details for you. Instead, you need to focus on the definition of the classes and the way they relate to each other from an object-oriented standpoint. Developers have different philosophies on the best way to go about defining a Hibernate domain model. Some developers believe it is best to define a database schema first and then create the classes to match the database structure. Obviously, there is no incorrect way (provided your application works reliably) to go about this process. However, in our experience, we have achieved the best results by defining the Hibernate mappings first, allowing you to consider the Java classes and the database table structure in tandem.

With Java 5 and Hibernate 3, the definition of Hibernate mapping files in XML is no longer necessary. Of course, you are welcome to continue following this more verbose methodology, and for many developers, externalizing the specifics of the database mapping is very much a good thing. However, it is hard to argue the fact that using Hibernate's new annotation support is easier and far less verbose. But please be aware that using annotations isn't your only (nor necessarily best) option.

Building the Comment and ArtEntity Java Classes

We've already described a few of our sample application's core entities, along with their corresponding associations. Now that we've considered how these entities will be represented in the database, let's start building our Java classes. Lets first define the Comment class:

```java
@Entity
public class Comment implements Serializable {
    private Long id;
    private String comment;
    private ArtEntity commentedArt;
    private Date commentDate;
    private String firstName;
    private String lastName;;
    private Integer version;

    @Id
    @GeneratedValue
    public Long getId() {
        return id;
    }

    public void setId(Long id) {
        this.id = id;
    }

    @ManyToOne
    public ArtEntity getCommentedArt() {
        return commentedArt;
    }
```

```java
public void setCommentedArt(
        ArtEntity commentedArt) {
    this.commentedArt = commentedArt;
}

@Temporal
public Date getCommentDate() {
    return commentDate;
}

public void setCommentDate(Date commentDate) {
    this.commentDate = commentDate;
}

@Version
public Integer getVersion() {
    return version;
}

public void setVersion(Integer version) {
    this.version = version;
}
}
```

Next, let's define the ArtEntity class:

```java
@Entity
public class ArtEntity implements Serializable {
    private Long id;
    private String title;
    private String subTitle;
    private Date uploadedDate;
    private Date displayDate;
    private Integer width;
    private Integer height;
    private String media;
    private String description;
    private String caption;
```

```java
private String imagePath;
private Boolean isGeneralViewable;
private Boolean isPrivilegeViewable;
private Set<Category> categories = new HashSet();
private Set<Comment> comments = new HashSet();

private Integer version;

public ArtEntity() {
}

@Id
@GeneratedValue
public Long getId() {
    return id;
}

public void setId(Long id) {
  this.id = id;
}

public Date getUploadedDate() {
  return uploadedDate;
}

public void setUploadedDate(Date uploadedDate) {
  this.uploadedDate = uploadedDate;
}

public Date getDisplayDate() {
  return displayDate;
}

public void setDisplayDate(Date displayDate) {
  this.displayDate = displayDate;
}

@ManyToMany(mappedBy = "artEntities")
```

```java
    public Set<Category> getCategories() {
       return categories;
    }

    public void setCategories(Set<Category> categories){
       this.categories = categories;
    }

    @OneToMany
    public Set<Comment> getComments() {
       return comments;
    }

    public void setComments(Set<Comment> comments) {
       this.comments = comments;
    }

    @Version
    public Integer getVersion() {
       return version;
    }

    public void setVersion(Integer version) {
       this.version = version;
    }

    public boolean addCommentToArt(Comment comment) {
       comment.setCommentedArt(this);
       return this.getComments().add(comment);
    }
 }
```

We've omitted some of the redundant getters and setters to conserve space. However, you'll immediately recognize that we're essentially defining a JavaBean or POJO—there are no references to Hibernate dependencies and no parent class from which to extend. We have defined the properties that we need to persist in the database along with their respective getters and setters. The simplicity of Hibernate's annotation support stems from using sensible defaults, as well as Hibernate's ability to infer associations and database field types by considering the Java type of each JavaBean property. When mappings are defined in XML, we must explicitly delineate the details of each property and association. Because annotations are embedded into code, we have the benefit of drawing hints from the code itself, which dramatically simplifies configuration efforts.

In addition to the appropriate getters and setters, notice that we have also added an `addCommentToArt(Comment comment)` method. This is a convenience for bidirectional associations, since it is important that references are set on both sides of the association. In the previously mentioned `addCommentToArt(Comment comment)` method, we ensure that the specified `comment` parameter is added to the `ArtEntity`'s comment collection and that the `comment`'s `commentedArt` property properly references the `ArtEntity` instance.

Exploring the Annotations

The key annotation for Hibernate persistence is `@Entity`. This annotation tells Hibernate that we intend to persist this class. If we were following the XML mapping approach, we would then need to define each field explicitly in the `hbm.xml` mapping file. With Hibernate annotations, it is really only necessary to define the associations and the exceptions to the rule. By default, Hibernate assumes each field should be persisted and will map it to the appropriate column in the database.

Hibernate will look at each property's Java type as well as its name and use this metadata to define a column's field type and field name respectively. We only need to specify those details that don't fall into Hibernate default behavior. For instance, if we don't want certain fields persisted, we need to specify that these properties are transient using the `@Transient` annotation. Similarly, if we want to veer from the default Hibernate naming conventions, we can explicitly specify the name of a particular column within an annotation.

This concept of sensible defaults, or convention over configuration, really reduces the amount of coding required to get a domain model up and running. Nevertheless, Hibernate annotation support still provides ample flexibility to override any of the default behavior, should we be so inclined. For instance, if we would like to define a table name for our Comment class that is different than the Java class name, we can accomplish this feat by using the @Table annotation:

```
@Table(name = "HOGWASH")
class Comment {
    . . . (Methods Omitted)
}
```

In a similar fashion, we can require that the comment property maps to the column commentText by using the @Column annotation:

```
@Comment(name = "commentText")
public String getComment() {
    return this.commentText;
}
```

This level of customization is very useful but most of the time is unnecessary and redundant (unless you are mapping your domain model to a legacy database). You should have a very good reason to override any of Hibernate's default behavior. If you feel the need to map a Java property to a column of a different name, you may want to reconsider your naming conventions. Now, it's not wrong to have discrepancies between column names and Java property names, but simplicity of configuration is very important, and we encourage you to limit the overriding of default behavior whenever possible. After all, less code equals less maintenance.

Hibernate annotation support does require that you define a primary key and all of your JavaBeans' associations. In the preceding example, you will notice that we have added the @Id annotation above the getId() method in our `Comment` class. This annotation tells Hibernate that the `id` property of our `Comment` class is the identifier (or primary key) for our `Comment` entity.

Below the `@Id` annotation, you will notice an annotation called `@GeneratedValue`. This annotation specifies the way in which a given instance's identifier will be created. The default scenario is AUTO, and in our example, this is the identifier generation strategy Hibernate will use (since we haven't defined a strategy at all). AUTO will look at the underlying database to make the decision as to how identifiers should be created. The options are to use a sequence, an identity column, or a special table for generating new IDs. If you wanted to override the default behavior and use a sequence, your `@GeneratedValue` annotation might look like this:

```
@GeneratedValue( ↰
    strategy=GenerationType.SEQUENCE, ↰
    generator="COMMENT_ID_SEQ")
```

This would create a sequence named COMMENT_ID_SEQ to be used for generating new IDs for our `Comment` table. Again, it is often easier to stick with the default ID generation strategy, but we have found that creating explicit sequences for each table is frequently a little cleaner. When using the AUTO mode for ID generation, Hibernate will pick the ideal strategy based on the database you are using. However, for many databases, Hibernate will end up creating a single sequence to use across all your tables. This can get a bit messy, and so we do recommend specifying a different sequence for each table or class if your domain model has some complexity to it. Hibernate offers many more options for a domain class's identifier, including Universally Unique Identifier (UUID)–based generation, or simply allowing your application to assign identifiers directly.

The next annotation in our `Comment` domain entity is the `@ManyToOne` annotation. This tells Hibernate that the `commentedArt` property will have a many-to-one association to the `ArtEntity` table. From a database perspective, specifying a `@ManyToOne` annotation on the comment field will add a foreign key field on our `Comment` table to the `ArtEntity` table. This also demonstrates some of the advantages of using Hibernate to architect both your domain model and your database schema. If Hibernate is utilized to generate your schema, it will also create foreign key constraints for your associations to ensure the referential integrity of your database is not compromised.

Using Cascading Options to Establish Data Relationships

Hibernate's association annotations also provide a great deal of flexibility. Most important of these customization options is `Cascade`. This brings us to a key feature of many ORM frameworks such as Hibernate. Associations within a domain model represent how different domain entities relate to one another. Often, these relationships can be expressed in layman's terms as parent-child relationships, meaning that one entity owns or encapsulates a collection of another entity. Within the database, associations are represented through table joins, but there is no clear analogue for representing the more hierarchical relationships we have within Java. This is where Hibernate comes in. Cascading options help to establish parent-child relationships, or more precisely, the rules for how save and delete options affecting one entity should *cascade* to associated entities.

For example, within our gallery application, we would assert that `ArtEntity` owns a collection of `Comment` instances. This is logical since a `Comment` is *attached* to a particular `ArtEntity` instance: an end user can post a comment about a particular image, and this comment is typically only relevant to the image about which it was posted. Furthermore, should an `ArtEntity` instance be deleted, it wouldn't make sense to keep its related `Comments` around anymore. In essence, comments are children of an `ArtEntity`.

We've just established several critical cascading rules about the `ArtEntity`-`Comment` relationship. Since, comments can be considered children of an `ArtEntity`, we can assert that a save operation invoked on an `ArtEntity` should also cascade to any added or updated `Comment` instances associated to that `ArtEntity` instance. Additionally, should an `ArtEntity` be deleted, we would want the delete action to cascade to any associated `Comment` instances. We can represent these cascading rules using the following annotation:

```
@OneToMany(cascade =
{javax.persistence.CascadeType.ALL})
  @Cascade(
{org.hibernate.annotations.CascadeType.SAVE_UPDATE,
org.hibernate.annotations.CascadeType.DELETE_ORPHAN})
  public Set<Comment> getComments() {
    return comments;
  }
}
```

We are actually using two types of annotations in this example: Hibernate and JPA (which we'll cover in the next chapter). Hibernate offers more fine-grained control over persistence than JPA. In this case, we are specifying the `CascadeType` of `Delete_Orphan`, which will also ensure that any dereferenced comments will also get deleted. We also specify a `CascadeType` of `Save_Update`, which will ensure save and update operations invoked on an `ArtEntity` instance will be passed along to child `Comment` instances as well.

Lazy Loading with Hibernate

Hibernate also offers control over fetching associations, allowing related entities to be lazily loaded when needed, rather than when the originating object is loaded from the database. This has dramatic performance benefits (if used properly) but can also cause even worse performance implications if you're not careful.

Hibernate also allows entities as well as association collections (e.g., a group of comments) to be implicitly cached. With caching enabled, Hibernate will first try to find an entity or collection in the cache before trying to query the database. Since loading data from the cache is far less expensive than a database operation, caching is another effective strategy for improving application performance. Hibernate integrates with several caching frameworks, such as EHCache and provides a `CacheManager` interface if you want to add your own caching solution. Once integrated, caching happens implicitly, without requiring any additional coding, other than specifying caching rules for each entity and collection. We'll cover caching in Chapter 8, but to get basic caching enabled on our domain model, we can add the following annotation to each domain entity, as well as its corresponding collections, to ensure they are appropriately cached:

```
@Entity
@Cache(usage =
CacheConcurrencyStrategy.NONSTRICT_READ_WRITE)
public class ArtEntity implements Serializable {

. . . Methods Omitted . . .

@OneToMany(cascade =
{javax.persistence.CascadeType.ALL})
  @Cascade(
{org.hibernate.annotations.CascadeType.SAVE_UPDATE,
org.hibernate.annotations.CascadeType.DELETE_ORPHAN})
  @Cache(usage =
CacheConcurrencyStrategy.NONSTRICT_READ_WRITE)
  public Set<Comment> getComments() {
    return comments;
  }
```

```
public void setComments(Set<Comment> comments) {
   this.comments = comments;
}

. . . Methods Omitted . . .
}
```

Specifying a read-write caching strategy ensures that Hibernate will invalidate the cache whenever a particular domain instance is updated. This prevents stale data from being stored in the cache. Caching details should be adjusted using the configuration file appropriate for the caching implementation you have selected. In the case of EHCache, you can configure specifics, such as the time-to-live (TTL) and cache size on a domain-by-domain basis within the ehcache.xml file. It is also important to point out that there are three types of caching options for Hibernate: domain, collection, and query. Domain and collection caching are demonstrated in the preceding example. Query caching is also a very powerful optimization technique, allowing the results of a particular query (given a unique set of query parameters) to be cached.

Rounding Out the Domain Model

We now need to define the rest of the classes in our domain model. We won't include the entire source code for our domain model here. However, please feel free to download the example code for this chapter if you would like to follow along. For our gallery application, we require a few more classes to help provide the persistence details for all of the gallery's functionality. We have already introduced the Person, Exhibition, and ArtEntity classes. As a quick recap, here is an overview of our domain model, as it currently stands:

- `Person`: Represents an administrative user or a registered user of our gallery application

- `Exhibition`: Organizes collections of images into logical groups

- `ArtEntity`: Represents an image in the application and contains metadata about the image, as well as its location

- `Comment`: Represents an individual comment that relates to a particular `ArtEntity` instance

Our `ArtEntity` class represents basic metadata about an image, but what if we need to store an image in different resolutions, such as thumbnails, medium, and high-resolution versions? We could certainly insert additional fields into our `ArtEntity` class, but Hibernate provides a cleaner solution.

Using Polymorphism with Hibernate

ORM solutions like Hibernate go far beyond mapping database fields to domain model instances. Object-oriented concepts, such as polymorphism, are also enabled by Hibernate and are an effective means for establishing a hierarchy of domain objects that share a set of core properties and functionality. Rather than store an image path directly within our `ArtEntity` class, let's instead refactor this data into a separate base class called `ArtData`. We will then create three subclasses that each extend the `ArtData` class (and therefore share its properties) but are tailored to represent a particular type of image. We will define the following four new domain classes:

- `ArtData`

- `ArtData_Gallery`

- `ArtData_Thumbnail`

- `ArtData_Storage`

The bulk of the properties will be stored within `ArtData`, since it is the base class. `ArtData_Thumbnail` will be used to represent thumbnails, while `ArtData_Storage` will persist a high-resolution version of the image, suitable for archival purposes or for zoomed-in views. `ArtData_Gallery` will be used to represent the standard view of an image within the gallery listing pages.

Hibernate provides two different options for implementing polymorphism: table-per-hierarchy and table-per-subclass. You can probably infer from the names how these two options differ.

Table-per-hierarchy combines all the properties of the class hierarchy into a single table, using a discriminator field to help determine which Java type is represented by each row in the database. The advantage of this approach is that all the necessary fields for any class within the hierarchy are included in a single table, without requiring the overhead of a database join. The disadvantage is that the design is not very normalized, and for any given type, there will likely be fields that will not be utilized.

The other option is table-per-subclass. In this scenario, each Java type is represented by a different table. To share properties across a Java hierarchy, tables are joined together. The advantage of this approach is that the design is clean and normalized. However, the overhead of joining tables will incur a performance hit.

Adding the ArtData Base Class

Which option to use really depends on your domain model. If there isn't too much disparity across classes within your class hierarchy, the table-per-hierarchy option probably makes the most sense. In our case, this is the option we will follow. Lets take a look at the base `ArtData` entity:

```
@Entity
@Inheritance(strategy=InheritanceType.SINGLE_TABLE)
@DiscriminatorColumn(
    discriminatorType = DiscriminatorType.STRING)
```

```java
@DiscriminatorValue("GENERIC")
public class ArtData implements Serializable {
  private Long id;
  private byte[] picture;
  private Integer version;

  public ArtData() {

  }

  public ArtData(byte[] picture) {
    this.picture = picture;
  }

  @Id
  @GeneratedValue
  public Long getId() {
    return id;
  }

  public void setId(Long id) {
    this.id = id;
  }

  public byte[] getPicture() {
    return picture;
  }

  public void setPicture(byte[] picture) {
    this.picture = picture;
  }

  @Version
  public Integer getVersion() {
    return version;
  }

  public void setVersion(Integer version) {
```

```
    this.version = version;
  }
}
```

Much of this class should already look familiar: you should notice the standard JavaBean conventions, as well as the core Hibernate annotations. Let's focus on the annotations that enable the inheritance in our model:

```
@Inheritance(strategy=InheritanceType.SINGLE_TABLE)
```

This annotation tells Hibernate that we want to utilize inheritance and that we are defining our base class. We are also specifying that we intend to use the table-per-hierarchy strategy (meaning that we want to persist all the fields within the entire hierarchy within a single table).

The @DiscriminatorColumn annotation provides Hibernate with the details about our discriminator. As mentioned earlier, the discriminator provides Hibernate with the clues it needs to infer to which Java type a particular database row corresponds. In our example, we are defining our discriminator column to be a String type. We could also use a char or an Integer.

Last, we define the discriminator value that each type will use through the @DiscriminatorValue annotation. In the case of the ArtData base class, we specify a value of GENERIC. So, for each ArtData instance that is persisted to the database, Hibernate will set the discriminator column to a value of GENERIC.

Adding the ArtData Child Classes

Finally, we must define the classes that extend from our ArtData base class. Each class is fairly similar to one another in our scenario, but inheritance provides a clean way to classify the different types of images within our gallery application. Furthermore, this approach also provides future extension points, should we need to define additional metadata that only relates to a particular image type, such as a thumbnail aspect ratio, or archival details for our `ArtData_Storage` class. As an example, lets take a look at our `ArtData_Thumbnail` class:

```
@Entity
@DiscriminatorValue("THUMBNAIL")
public class ArtData_Thumbnail
    extends ArtData implements Serializable {

  public ArtData_Thumbnail(byte[] picture) {
    this.setPicture(picture);
  }

  public ArtData_Thumbnail() {
  }
}
```

This is a fairly straightforward class. Notice, however, that we've set a discriminator value of THUMBNAIL.

Let's look at our `ArtEntity` class again, now with all of our refactorings applied:

```
@Entity
public class ArtEntity implements Serializable {
  private Long id;
  private String title;
  private String subTitle;
  private Date uploadedDate;
  private Date displayDate;
  private Integer width;
  private Integer height;
  private String media;
  private String description;
  private String caption;
  private ArtData_Gallery galleryPicture;
  private ArtData_Storage storagePicture;
  private ArtData_Thumbnail thumbnailPicture;
  private Boolean isGeneralViewable;
  private Boolean isPrivilegeViewable;
```

```java
private Set<Category> categories = new HashSet();
private Set<Comment> comments = new HashSet();
private Integer version;
public ArtEntity() {

}
@Id
@GeneratedValue

public Long getId() {
  return id;
}

public void setId(Long id) {
  this.id = id;
}

@OneToOne(cascade = CascadeType.ALL)
@JoinColumn()
public ArtData_Gallery getGalleryPicture() {
  return galleryPicture;
}

public void setGalleryPicture(ArtData_Gallery pic){
  this.galleryPicture = pic;
}

@OneToOne(cascade = CascadeType.ALL)
@JoinColumn()
public ArtData_Storage getStoragePicture() {
  return storagePicture;
}

  public void setStoragePicture(ArtData_Storage pic) {
  this.storagePicture = pic;
}

@OneToOne(cascade = CascadeType.ALL)
```

```java
@JoinColumn()
public ArtData_Thumbnail getThumbnailPicture() {
  return thumbnailPicture;
}

public void setThumbnailPicture(
    ArtData_Thumbnail pic) {
  this.thumbnailPicture = pic;
}

public String getTitle() {
  return title;
}

public void setTitle(String title) {
  this.title = title;
}

public String getSubTitle() {
  return subTitle;
}

@Temporal
public Date getUploadedDate() {
  return uploadedDate;
}

public void setUploadedDate(Date uploadedDate) {
  this.uploadedDate = uploadedDate;
}

@Temporal
public Date getDisplayDate() {
  return displayDate;
}

public void setDisplayDate(Date displayDate) {
  this.displayDate = displayDate;
```

```
    }

    public void setHeight(Integer height) {
      this.height = height;
    }

    @ManyToMany(mappedBy = "artEntities")
    public Set<Category> getCategories() {
      return categories;
    }

    @OneToMany
    public Set<Comment> getComments() {
      return comments;
    }

    public void setComments(Set<Comment> comments) {
      this.comments = comments;
    }

    @Version
    public Integer getVersion() {
      return version;
    }

  }
```

You will notice that we have now defined a few one-to-one relationships
for our thumbnailPicture, galleryPicture, and storagePicture
properties. To simplify our code, we defined three separate one-to-one
associations. However, we could have also chosen to put all the ArtData
entities into a single collection, with a generic type of the ArtData base
class. Since each image type is represented by a different subclass, it would
be easy to differentiate between the different image types.

Also, notice that we have defined a many-to-many association to the
Category class for the categories property. We have also added the

mappedBy hint here to indicate that the inverse side of this relationship is referenced by the artEntities property in the Comment class. For bidirectional many-to-many associations, we need to tell Hibernate which side of the collection is the owner. By adding the mappedBy attribute to the Comment class, we are asserting that the Category class owns the relationship.

Building the DAOs

Now that we've described our key domain classes, lets begin building our DAOs, starting with the CategoryDao. As we mentioned earlier, ArtEntity classes can be organized into one or more categories. This feature allows end users to browse for photos and artwork by categories. The CategoryDao interface can be defined as follows:

```
public interface CategoryDao {
   public List<Category> getCategories()
       throws DataAccessException;
   public Category getCategory(Long catId)
       throws DataAccessException;
   public List<ArtEntity> getArtworkInCategory(
       Long catId) throws DataAccessException;
   public void saveCategory(Category category)
       throws DataAccessException;
}
```

These methods allow us to load an individual category, find all the categories, and find artwork within a particular category. The CategoryDao allows us to save new instances of Category objects as well.

Now that we've defined an interface, let's move on to the implementation:

```
public class CategoryDaoImpl
   extends HibernateDaoSupport implements CategoryDao {

   public List<Category> getCategories()
```

```
        throws DataAccessException {
    return this.getHibernateTemplate().find(
      "select categories from Category categories"
    );
  }

  public Category getCategory(Long catId)
          throws DataAccessException {
    return (Category) this.getHibernateTemplate()
        .load(Category.class, catId);
  }

  public List<ArtEntity> getArtworkInCategory(Long id)
          throws DataAccessException {
    return
        this.getHibernateTemplate().findByNamedParam(
          "select art from Category cat " +
          "join cat.artEntities art "+
          "where cat.id = :catId ",
          "catId", catId
        );
  }

  public void saveCategory(Category category)
          throws DataAccessException {
    this.getHibernateTemplate()
        .saveOrUpdate(category);
  }
}
}
```

Building the Hibernate DAO Layer Using Spring

Spring excels at reducing the amount of code you need to write in order to get something to work. When it comes to building Hibernate DAO classes, there are several options. The easiest solution is to extend Spring's HibernateDaoSupport class. This abstract class requires that you pass in a Hibernate SessionFactory via the setSessionFactory(SessionFactory sessionFactory) setter method. You should, of course, configure your SessionFactory in Spring so that it can be easily injected via configuration. We will demonstrate this process shortly.

When a valid SessionFactory is passed in to a class that extends HibernateDaoSupport, a HibernateTemplate instance is automatically created for you. The HibernateTemplate works in a very similar fashion to the JDBCTemplate examples illustrated in the previous chapter. Following the template design pattern, this class handles all the heavy lifting required by Hibernate so that you can focus on the persistence logic. The result is clean code that usually reflects very little other than the Hibernate persistence operations you are attempting.

Extending the HibernateDaoSupport class is ideal for reducing code, since it automatically defines a setter for your Hibernate SessionFactory and handles the creation of a HibernateTemplate. However, if your DAO needs to extend from a different base class, you won't be able to extend HibernateDaoSupport as well. Of course, flexibility and decoupling are key Spring philosophies, therefore you are rarely required to extend from framework classes (although this is sometimes preferred). Instead, you can simply create your HibernateTemplate directly:

```
public class CategoryDaoImpl implements CategoryDao {
private SessionFactory sessionFactory;
private HibernateTemplate hibernateTemplate;

public void setSessionFactory(
        SessionFactory sessionFactory) {
  this.sessionFactory = sessionFactory;
  this.hibernateTemplate =
    new HibernateTemplate(sessionFactory);
  }
}
```

This approach requires a little more plumbing, but you are now free from extending any framework-specific classes. Notice that we have chosen to create our `HibernateTemplate` within our `setSessionFactory(SessionFactory sf)` setter method. This way, when Spring injects the Hibernate `SessionFactory`, the `HibernateTemplate` will be automatically created.

Enabling Query Caching with the HibernateTemplate

The `HibernateTemplate` includes two methods needed to facilitate query caching. As mentioned earlier, using a query cache with Hibernate can provide a significant performance boost by minimizing the number of trips to the database. There are several different strategies for enabling query caching. The option we recommend most is to configure a `HibernateTemplate` directly in your Spring configuration. This way, you can externalize and centralize query-cache specifics:

```
<bean id="hibernateTemplate"
    class="org.springframework.orm ↪
    .hibernate3.HibernateTemplate">
  <property name="sessionFactory"
    ref="sessionFactory"/>
  <property name="queryCacheRegion"
    value="querycache_artwork"/>
  <property name="cacheQueries" value="true"/>
</bean>
```

You can then inject this preconfigured `HibernateTemplate` directly into your DAO implementation. If your DAO extends from the `HibernateDaoSupport` class, it will use the `SessionFactory` applied to your Spring-configured `HibernateTemplate` automatically. Using this strategy, you can ensure that query caching is enabled for all operations that make use of the `HibernateTemplate`. An alternative approach is to

configure query-caching details in code through extending
`HibernateTemplate` or setting the query cache specifics directly.

Creating Our Category DAO Implementation

Let's now discuss how our `CategoryDaoImpl` class works. Just like our
`JDBCTemplate` examples, we don't have to worry about low-level details;
most Hibernate operations can be handled through the
`HibernateTemplate`. When working with Hibernate directly, you
normally are required to create a new Hibernate `Session` from a
`SessionFactory`. For most operations, you also need to be concerned with
transactional details, ensuring that transactions are started at the beginning
of an operation and then either committed or rolled back when the
operation completes. The `HibernateTemplate` (along with other Spring
framework classes) will ensure that the Hibernate `Session` is opened and
closed and that transactional semantics are properly applied and
propagated. We are free to specify transactional requirements all in code.
However, doing so can be verbose and error prone. Instead, we will specify
our transactional requirements entirely via configuration, separating
transactional details from our persistence logic. This is one of the key
purposes of the service facade layer, which we will discuss shortly.

Using a `HibernateTemplate` is not the only valid approach, when using
Spring and Hibernate together. If your DAO extends from the
`HibernateDaoSupport` class, you may simply call the
`getSession(boolean allowcreate)` method. This will return a
Hibernate `Session`, allowing you to work directly with the core Hibernate
API methods. This approach will provide you with a little more flexibility
than using the `HibernateTemplate`, while still allowing your code to
work with Spring's generic `DataAccess` exception hierarchy. However,
you will usually find `HibernateTemplate` a cleaner and simpler strategy.

We will come back to transactional support shortly. Now, let's look at how the `HibernateTemplate` is used. Our first method in the `CategoryDaoImpl` class is defined as following:

```
public List<Category> getCategories()
    throws DataAccessException {
  return this.getHibernateTemplate().find(
    "select categories from Category categories"
   );
}
```

This method simply loads all `Category` instances from the database. To accomplish this, we use the `HibernateTemplate`'s `find` method. This method has numerous permutations, allowing for the specification of different queries and types of parameters. This version simply takes a Hibernate Query Language (HQL) query with no parameters. For the purposes of loading all categories from the database, this is perfect. However, for most HQL queries, we will need to be able to specify named parameters.

Note We recommend that you never place HQL queries directly within the DAO. Instead, use one of the permutations of `findByNamedQuery`. . . methods. Doing so allows you to centralize your HQL queries within Hibernate mapping files or within domain class files using the `@NamedQuery` annotation. Keeping named queries within mapping files also allows you to tweak your HQL queries without having to recompile your classes.

Using HQL Queries

Let's jump ahead to the finder method that gets all `ArtEntity` instances within a particular `Category`:

```
public List<ArtEntity> getArtworkInCategory(Long catId)
    throws DataAccessException {
  return this.getHibernateTemplate().findByNamedParam(
```

```
        "select art from Category cat " +
        "join cat.artEntities art " +
        "where cat.id = :catId ",
        "catId", catId
    );
}
```

This method uses a more complex HQL query that joins `Category` with `ArtEntity`, specifying a *where* condition with a parameterized `CategoryId`. For this method, we are using `HibernateTemplate`'s `findByNamedParam` method. Notice that this method takes three parameters: the HQL query, the HQL parameter name, and the parameter itself. We always recommend using named parameters instead of positional parameters to make your code significantly clearer. Notice that our HQL query specifies the condition `where cat.id = :catId`. The `catId` is Hibernate's way of defining a named parameter in your query. This name can then be referenced as the parameter name to `HibernateTemplate`'s `findByNamedParam` method.

In the preceding example, we only have a single parameter, but this is often not the case. In situations in which we require more than a single HQL parameter, we can use the overloaded version of `findByNamedParam` that takes a `String` array (as the second parameter) to define the parameter names we are passing into our finder method and an `Object` array for the actual parameter values. This more flexible version works about the same as the preceding example except the second and third parameters both take arrays instead of a `String` and an `Object` respectively. For instance, let's take a look at our `authenticatePerson` method in the `PersonDaoImpl` class:

```
public Person authenticatePerson(String username,
    String password)
    throws DataAccessException, AuthenticationException {
    List<Person> validUsers = this.getHibernateTemplate()
        .findByNamedParam(
```

```
    "select people from Person people where" +
    "people.username = :username " +
    "and people.password = :password",
     new String[] {"username", "password"},
     new String[] {username, password }
   );
 if (validUsers == null || validUsers.size() <= 0)
   throw new AuthenticationException(
     "No users found");
 return validUsers.get(0);
}
```

In the preceding example, we are passing two conditions to our HQL query: username and password. Notice that the second argument contains a String array of HQL parameter names, while the third method argument takes a String array of values. The HibernateTemplate also offers overloaded alternatives, in which you can specify an object or object array for parameter values, allowing you to use any Java type as parameter value in an HQL query.

So, you now understand how to perform a few types of HQL queries in Hibernate with Spring. We should also point out that Hibernate offers another powerful strategy for querying using the Criteria API. However we won't be covering this alternative querying approach in this book. But how do we simply load an object by ID? Our CategoryDao defines a simple getCategoryById method the following way:

```
return (Category) this.getHibernateTemplate()
   .load(Category.class, catId
);
```

This seems simple enough. We call HibernateTemplate's load method, passing in the class that represents the type of entity we wish to load, followed by the object's identifier. Calling load will access an object using Session.load(Class, Serializable). This method will trigger an exception if no entity with the given identifier exists. However, if you are working with the `HibernateTemplate`, the method will trigger an unchecked `DataAccessException`, since Hibernate exceptions will be converted to Spring's consistent `DataAccessException` hierarchy. Another approach is Hibernate's `Session.get(Class, Serializable)` method. This approach works in a similar manner but will only return `null` (instead of throwing an exception) if the entity does not exist in the database.

Persisting Data with Hibernate

Now that we've discussed a few options for defining finder methods using `HibernateTemplate`, how do we actually persist data? Our `CategoryDaoImpl` class defines a save method for the `Category` instance as follows:

```
public void saveCategory(Category category)
          throws DataAccessException {
  this.getHibernateTemplate().saveOrUpdate(category);
}
```

Using `HibernateTemplate`'s `saveOrUpdate` is similar to calling `Session.saveOrUpdate(Object)` using the core Hibernate API. There are also other saving options available in the `HibernateTemplate`, such as merge, save, and update, if you want more specific kinds of persisting behavior.

Now that we've defined the `CategoryDao` implementation, let's take a look at the Spring configuration behind the scenes.

Let's begin with the datasource. This configuration is identical to our Spring JDBC sample in our previous chapter. In fact, this makes sharing a datasource between Spring JDBC and Hibernate fairly trivial. Lets look at the configuration in more detail:

```xml
<beans
xmlns="http://www.springframework.org/schema/beans"
xmlns:xsi="http://www.w3.org/2001/XMLSchema-instance"
xmlns:context="http://www.springframework.org/
schema/context"
xmlns:aop="http://www.springframework.org/schema/aop"
xmlns:p="http://www.springframework.org/schema/p"
xmlns:tx="http://www.springframework.org/schema/tx"
xsi:schemaLocation="http://www.springframework.org/
schema/beans
http://www.springframework.org/schema/beans/
spring-beans-2.5.xsd
http://www.springframework.org/schema/context
http://www.springframework.org/schema/context/
spring-context-2.5.xsd
http://www.springframework.org/schema/tx
http://www.springframework.org/schema/tx/
spring-tx-2.5.xsd
http://www.springframework.org/schema/aop
http://www.springframework.org/schema/aop/
spring-aop-2.5.xsd">

  <!-- ==== GENERAL DEFINITIONS  -->
<context:property-placeholder
  location="classpath:jdbc.properties"/>


<!-- ===== RESOURCE DEFINITIONS  -->

<!-- Local DataSource that works in any environment -->
<bean id="dataSource"
class="org.springframework.jdbc.datasource
.DriverManagerDataSource"
  p:driverClassName="${jdbc.driverClassName}"
  p:url="${jdbc.url}"
  p:username="${jdbc.username}"
  p:password="${jdbc.password}"/>
```

```xml
<!-- JNDI DataSource for J2EE environments -->
<import resource="spring-hibernate.xml"/>

  <context:component-scan
    base-package="com.smartpants.artwork.service">
    <context:include-filter type="annotation"
    expression=
      "org.springframework.stereotype.Service"/>
  </context:component-scan>

  </beans>
</bean>
```

This configuration defines a `PropertyPlaceHolderConfigurer`, which allows us to externalize the specifics of our database configuration to a properties file outside the Spring configuration. This detail isn't necessary, but it makes our configuration more portable, since we can easily define different database configurations for different machines and platforms— without having to change our Spring configuration. For instance, here is a snippet of our `jdbc.properties` file:

```
jdbc.driverClassName=org.hsqldb.jdbcDriver

jdbc.url=jdbc:hsqldb:mem:artwork
jdbc.username=sa
jdbc.password=

hibernate.dialect=org.hibernate.dialect.HSQLDialect

hibernate.connection.provider_class= ↪
org.connection.C3P0ConnectionProvider
hibernate.transaction.factory_class= ↪
org.transaction.JDBCTransactionFactory
hibernate.cache.provider_class= ↪
org.hibernate.cache.EhCacheProvider
hibernate.show_sql=false
```

```
hibernate.jdbc.batch_size=5
```

The syntax is intuitive: each line contains a simple expression, in which the left side represents the property name and the right side (after the =) represents the configured value. This externalization makes it very easy to swap different database configurations for different environments and better externalizes these details from application-specific configuration. Within the Spring configuration, we can utilize placeholder references through the use of the `${}` notation. These placeholders represent external values stored in our datasource properties file, injected into our configuration file, courtesy of our `PropertyPlaceholderConfigurer`.

Using import Statements

After the `placeholder` configurer, you'll notice that we define our datasource, using values derived from the `jdbc.properties` file illustrated previously. Below the datasource configuration is an `import` statement:

```
<import resource="spring-hibernate.xml"/>
```

Imports allow us to specify an external Spring configuration file to be integrated into your application configuration. This is a useful construct, especially in our demonstration application, as we can easily externalize the different persistence strategies, keeping each version in its own file that gets imported through the preceding line. However, we recommend that you carefully consider how Spring files get imported, as this can also be a cause for confusion (since exactly which Spring configurations are getting loaded isn't necessarily clear unless you examine each file carefully). A cleaner approach might be to specify all Spring configuration files that get loaded during the bootstrapping of your application.

Managing Transactions

In our example, we are importing the `spring-hibernate.xml` file, keeping all of our Hibernate configuration localized to a single file. This file contains all the Spring configuration required to create and configure a Hibernate `SessionFactory`, as well as to create a `TransactionManager`. We then apply transactional semantics to our service facade classes by annotating which methods need to be transactional (along with the transactional requirements, such as isolation level and whether the transaction is read-only).

Let's take a peek our the `spring-hibernate.xml` file:

```
<beans
 xmlns=http://www.springframework.org/schema/beans
 xmlns:xsi="http://www.w3.org/2001/XMLSchema-instance"
 xmlns:context=
"http://www.springframework.org/schema/context"
 xmlns:aop="http://www.springframework.org/ ↪
schema/aop"
 xmlns:p="http://www.springframework.org/schema/p"
 xmlns:tx="http://www.springframework.org/schema/tx"
 xsi:schemaLocation="
http://www.springframework.org/schema/beans
    http://www.springframework.org/schema/ ↪
beans/spring-beans-2.5.xsd
http://www.springframework.org/schema/context
    http://www.springframework.org/schema/ ↪
context/spring-context-2.5.xsd
http://www.springframework.org/schema/tx
    http://www.springframework.org/schema/ ↪
tx/spring-tx-2.5.xsd
http://www.springframework.org/schema/aop
    http://www.springframework.org/schema/ ↪
aop/spring-aop-2.5.xsd">
```

```xml
<!-- Hibernate SessionFactory -->
<bean id="sessionFactory"
class="org.springframework.orm.hibernate3. ↪
annotation.AnnotationSessionFactoryBean"
  p:dataSource-ref="dataSource"
  p:lobHandler-ref="defaultLobHandler">
  <property name="annotatedClasses">
    <list>
    <value>
      com.smartpants.artwork.domain.ArtData
    </value>
    <value>
      com.smartpants.artwork.domain.ArtData_Gallery
    </value>
    <value>
      com.smartpants.artwork.domain.ArtData_Storage
    </value>
    <value>
      com.smartpants.artwork.domain.ArtData_Thumbnail
    </value>
    <value>
      com.smartpants.artwork.domain.ArtEntity
    </value>
    <value>
      com.smartpants.artwork.domain.Category
    </value>
    <value>
      com.smartpants.artwork.domain.Comment
    </value>
    <value>
      com.smartpants.artwork.domain.Exhibition
    </value>
    <value>
      com.smartpants.artwork.domain.Person
    </value>
    </list>
  </property>
```

```xml
<property name="hibernateProperties">
  <value>
    hibernate.dialect=${hibernate.dialect}
    hibernate.jdbc.batch_size= ↪
${hibernate.jdbc.batch_size}
    hibernate.c3p0.max_size= ↪
${hibernate.c3p0.max_size}
    hibernate.c3p0.min_size= ↪
${hibernate.c3p0.min_size}
    hibernate.c3p0.timeout= ↪
${hibernate.c3p0.timeout}
    hibernate.c3p0.max_statements= ↪
${hibernate.c3p0.max_statements}
    hibernate.c3p0.idle_test_period= ↪
${hibernate.c3p0.idle_test_period}
    hibernate.c3p0.acquire_increment= ↪
${hibernate.c3p0.acquire_increment}
    hibernate.c3p0.validate= ↪
${hibernate.c3p0.validate}
    hibernate.cache.provider_class= ↪
${hibernate.cache.provider_class}
    hibernate.connection.provider_class= ↪
${hibernate.connection.provider_class}
    hibernate.show_sql=${hibernate.show_sql}
    hibernate.hbm2ddl.auto=update
hibernate.cache.use_second_level_cache=true
    hibernate.cache.use_query_cache=true
  </value>
</property>
</bean>

<!-- Database LOB Handling -->

<bean id="defaultLobHandler"
    class="org.springframework.jdbc.support. ↪
lob.DefaultLobHandler" />
```

```
<tx:annotation-driven
    transaction-manager="transactionManager"/>

<!-- Transaction manager -->
<bean id="transactionManager"
    class="org.springframework.orm. ↪
hibernate3.HibernateTransactionManager"
    p:sessionFactory-ref="sessionFactory"/>

<!-- Read in daos from the hibernate package -->
<context:component-scan base-package=
    "com.smartpants.artwork.dao.hibernate">
    <context:include-filter type="annotation"
        expression="org.springframework. ↪
stereotype.Repository"/>
</context:component-scan>

</beans>
```

Let's go through this configuration file, piece by piece. The first part (and bulk) of this file specifies the `SessionFactory`. We are declaring that we want to use the `AnnotationSessionFactoryBean`, which will allow us to use annotations as a means to describe the persistent properties of our domain layer (instead of Hibernate XML mapping files). We are using a `Factory-bean` in this case, meaning we aren't creating an instance of the `AnnotationSessionFactoryBean`, in this case, but are using the factory pattern, relying on the `AnnotationSessionFactoryBean` to create and configure a `SessionFactory` for us.

Notice that we have configured two list properties. The first list delineates each annotated domain class we wish to have this `SessionFactory` manage. The second list contains important Hibernate properties. You will notice that most of these properties contain values that follow the `${}` pattern, meaning this configuration data will be handled by our

`PropertyPlaceholderConfigurer` (using values from the `jdbc.properties` file).

Next, we configure a `defaultLobHandler` bean (which is also injected into the Hibernate `SessionFactory`). LOB handlers help to handle binary data (BLOBs and CLOBs) to and from the database. Many applications don't require BLOBs, so this bean may not be necessary. But since we are using our database to store our image data, defining a default `LobHandler` is important.

The next two beans are important for defining our `TransactionManager`:

```
<tx:annotation-driven
    transaction-manager="transactionManager"/>

    <!--
        Transaction manager for a single
        Hibernate SessionFactory (alternative to JTA)
    -->
<bean id="transactionManager"
    class="org.springframework.orm.hibernate3. ➥
HibernateTransactionManager"
    p:sessionFactory-ref="sessionFactory"/>
```

Here, we are using the `tx` namespace, specifying that we are going to be delineating transactional semantics within our service layer using annotations. This bean contains a `transaction-manager` attribute that requires an `id` for a `transactionManager` bean. This is defined next: we simply configure a bean with an `id` of `TransactionManager` and a `class` attribute that points to Spring's `HibernateTransactionManager`. We also inject a reference to our `SessionFactory` bean we defined at the beginning of our file.

The last bit of our configuration is a component scan:

```
<context:component-scan
    base-package="com.smartpants.artwork.dao.hibernate">
```

```
<context:include-filter type="annotation"
    expression=
    "org.springframework.stereotype.Repository"/>
</context:component-scan>
```

We discussed component scanning earlier, so you will recall that this is a powerful construct that allows Spring to search for classes within a package that contain `@Component` annotation. Typically, you will use the `@Repository`, `@Service`, or `@Controller` annotation (each of which logically extend from the `@Component` annotation), although you may also derive your own. In this case, we are telling Spring to search within the `com.smartpants.artwork.dao.hibernate` package and look for any classes that contain the `@Repository` annotation. `@Repository` typically represents classes that provide DAO functionality.

Jumping back to our `datamodel.xml` file (which contained the import of the Spring Hibernate file we just described), you will notice that we have another `Component` scan setup:

```
<context:component-scan
    base-package="com.smartpants.artwork.service">
        <context:include-filter type="annotation"
    expression="org.springframework.stereotype.Service"/>
</context:component-scan>
```

This bean looks very similar to the DAO scan in the Spring Hibernate file. However, this configuration declares that we are looking within the `com.smartpants.artwork.service` package and that we are only looking for classes annotated with the `@Service` annotation. `@Service` typically represents classes that serve as a transactional service facade layer.

Defining the Service Facade Layer

Now that we've gotten the configuration out of the way, lets define our service layer. Normally, you would likely create several service classes, using a similar differentiation strategy to the approach we used in defining our DAO layer. Lets begin with our scaffolding:

```
@Service(value = "artworkFacade")
@Transactional
public class ArtworkFacadeImpl ↪
            implements ArtworkFacade {
  private ArtworkDao artworkDao;
  private CategoryDao categoryDao;
  private ExhibitionDao exhibitionDao;
  private PersonDao personDao;


}
```

We start off by annotating our class with the `@Service` annotation. We specify a value of `artworkFacade` so that we can reference this bean directly within the Spring `ApplicationContext`. We have also added the `@Transactional` annotation, declaring that the methods within this class should all run within a transactional context.

With our scaffolding defined, we need to define some of our facade methods:

```
@Transactional(readOnly = true)
  public ArtEntity getArtEntity(Long id)
        throws DataAccessException {
    return artworkDao.getArtEntity(id);
  }

  @Transactional(readOnly = false)
  public void saveArtEntity(ArtEntity art)
      throws DataAccessException {
    artworkDao.saveArtEntity(art);
  }
```

So as not to be redundant, we won't define all of our service layer methods. We've included two important methods, however: one method that loads an `ArtEntity` by its primary key and another that saves an `ArtEntity`.

You will notice that we delegate to our `ArtworkDao` implementation to do most of the heavy lifting. Our example is somewhat basic; more often, service layer methods will delegate to multiple DAO methods to ensure that several database operations all occur within a single transaction. We can provide details to the `@Transactional` annotation above each method to control the transactional semantics. In the case of the `getArtEntity` method, we intend the transaction to be read-only. However, in our `SaveArtEntity` method, we specify that our transaction should not be read-only.

The `@Transactional` annotation is quite flexible and allows us to specify details such as the isolation level, timeout constraints, and propagation details. We can also specify which exceptions should or should not trigger a rollback. For instance, in the following contrived example (unrelated to our gallery application) we could require that the following service method occurs within a nested transaction and that it will be rolled back if a `CreditLimitExceededException` gets thrown but not if a `ScaryBankException` is thrown:

```
@Transactional(readOnly = false,
   propagation = Propagation.NESTED,
   rollbackFor = CreditLimitExceededException.class,
   noRollbackFor= ScaryBankException)
public Boolean transferFunds(double money){
   . . . implementation omitted . . .

}
```

The preceding scenario should give you a decent idea of how flexible Spring's transactional support can be. We will cover transactions in more detail in Chapter 6.

Although discussing application development outside the persistence tier is outside the scope of this book, it is important to understand where the service layer facade fits within a typical application. If you are developing a web application, your service classes would be injected into your controllers. The key point to take away here is that the service layer is usually the core API of your application; it's the business logic that describes an atomic action, or unit of work, that needs to be completed.

Summary

In this chapter, we've introduced some core ORM concepts, and you learned more about how Spring and Hibernate can be used together. We've also reinforced some key design patterns that are instrumental to the way in which Spring integrates with many persistence frameworks. Through our gallery application examples, we've described how a persistence tier can be architected, by first defining a domain model and then building a DAO and service facade. We've also seen multiple approaches for configuring and building a Hibernate `SessionFactory`, as well as a DAO and service layer.

In the next chapter, you will learn more about JPA, a standards-based persistence technology whose design was significantly influenced by Hibernate.

Chapter 4: Integrating JPA with Spring

The Java Persistence API (JPA) was the brainchild of the EJB 3.0 standardization committee. They produced the JPA specification for both EJB 3.0 entity bean definitions and for the ORM world at large. JPA is supported by various ORMs, including Hibernate, popular Java Data Object (JDO) implementations and, obviously, EJB 3.0 Entity Beans.

JPA has a set of annotations that can be applied to domain classes to map these objects to database tables and member variables to columns. JPA also features an SQL-like language called JPAQL that can query the database with an object-oriented flavor. To access your database-mapped domain model or to execute JPAQL queries, you use the `EntityManager`. `EntityManager` is an amalgamation of the Hibernate `SessionFactory` and `Session` objects that you learned about in Chapter 3. Simply speaking, Hibernate's `SessionFactory` is aware of global configuration details, while the `Session` scope is limited to the current transaction. The JPA `EntityManager` knows how to do both.

Chapter 3, the Hibernate chapter, covered quite a bit of the domain object annotations, such as `@Entity` and `@Id`. Most of the domain annotations you saw previously will apply to JPA as well, so we won't cover them in detail in this chapter. In this chapter, you'll learn a bit about JPAQL and `EntityManager` and how they interact with Spring. Mostly, you'll learn how to go about setting up JPA; configuring JPA is a bit more complicated than configuring Hibernate. We will also apply some of the concepts discussed in the previous two chapters, such as domain model and layering fundamentals.

Considering Configuration Options

JPA has a lot of configuration options. Because JPA is a big part of EJB, you can use an EJB container to configure JPA and expose the container's `EntityManger` to Spring. You can also configure JPA directly within Spring using one of the myriad JPA implementations that were mentioned earlier. One significant difference between JPA implementations that is important to know about is the need (or lack thereof) of something called *load-time weaving*, which is the type of byte-code manipulation required for AOP. Load-time weaving is needed for creating transactionally aware JPA `EntityManagers` and `Entity` objects that can perform lazy loading. EJB servers have their own load-time weaving mechanism and so does Spring.

A single `EntityManager` can handle this type of functionality only through the support of the level of indirection that a proxy can provide. Remember the "lack thereof" comment tossed in the previous paragraph? The Hibernate JPA implementation is one of the frameworks that doesn't require load-time weaving, so we'll use that implementation in this chapter to get you up and running in a JPA environment as quickly as possible.

Creating Your First JPA Application

In this chapter, we'll cover the basics of creating a JPA application with Hibernate. Our objective is to create the following scenario:

- A single entity
- Spring database configuration with an in memory database (HSQLDB)
- Spring-based Hibernate JPA configuration
- A JUnit unit test that will create a persisted entity and run a simple query against that entity

As with Hibernate, JPA allows us to specify how a Java class is mapped to the database via Java 5 annotations. The most important annotation is `@Entity`.

@Entity

A good portion of the JPA annotations were inspired by Hibernate's annotations. For example, adding an `@Entity` annotation to a POJO and an `@Id` annotation to an appropriate getter makes that POJO a persistable object! You've already seen this kind of approach in the Hibernate chapter, so we'll only create a basic example of an `@Entity` here using the `Person` POJO you saw in Chapter 1:

```
package com.smartpants.artwork.domain;
// imports
@Entity
public class Person implements Serializable {
    private Long id;

    private String firstName;
    private String lastName;
    private String username;
    private String password;
    private Integer roleLevel;
    @Id
    @GeneratedValue
    public Long getId() {
        return id;
    }
    public void setId(Long id) {
        this.id = id;
```

```
    }
    // implement the other get
    // Remember to implement equals and hashCode
        . . . Getters and Setters Omitted
    }
```

Note   The implements Serializable code that you see in the Person class isn't strictly necessary as far as the JPA specification is concerned. However, it is needed if you're going to use either EJB remoting or caching, both of which require objects to be Serializable.

The additions of the @Entity and @Id annotations allow the Person entity to be used as an EJB entity bean or in Hibernate or Eclipse Link (formerly known as Top Link). In those environments, this bean would map to a Person table. The addition of the @GeneratedValue annotation assures that the id column will be autogenerated. All of the other fields (firstName, lastName, username and password) will be mapped to similarly named VARCHAR or String columns.

Caution   equals and hashCode are tricky to implement. Your first reaction for equals and hashCode could be to just use the ID for comparison. That won't work if an object is added to an ordered Collection or a Map before it is saved, since the ID isn't populated until after it's saved to the database! Unfortunately, there really isn't a foolproof plan for equals and hashCode, so beware!

Besides @Entity and @Id, JPA has plenty of other annotations as well, including @Table, @Column, @GeneratedValue, @ManyToOne, @Inheritance, @DiscriminatorColumn, @DiscriminatorValue, @Version, @OneToOne, @JoinColumn, @Temporal, and @NamedQuery, which you saw in Chapter 3. JPA has quite a few other annotations you can apply to entity objects that we won't cover in this book.

We will, however, cover a few more JPA classes and annotations that we will need in order to make use of the entity objects we've created, specifically the `EntityManager` class and the `@PersistenceContext` annotation. Let's see how we can perform create, read, update, and delete (CRUD) operations using `EntityManager`.

Using EntityManager in CRUD Operations

We'll use JPA's `EntityManager` to CRUD operations. Let's create a DAO that saves and finds a `Person` entity. We'll start with the same interface that we introduced in Chapter 1:

```
public interface PersonDao {
    public Person getPerson(Long personId);
    public void savePerson(Person person);
    public List<Person> getPeople();
    public Person getPersonByUsername
      (String username)
        throws EntityNotFoundException;
    public Person authenticatePerson
      (String username, String password)
        throws AuthenticationException;
}
```

Here's a JPA implementation of the `PersonDao`:

```
project com.smartpants.artwork.dao.jpa;

// imports go here
@Repository
public class PersonDaoImpl implements PersonDao {

    private EntityManager em;

    @PersistenceContext
```

```
public setEntityManager(EntityManager em){
  this.em = em;
}

@Transactional(readOnly = true)
@SuppressWarnings("unchecked")
public Collection<Person> getPeople(){
  return this.em.createQuery(
    "SELECT person FROM Person person"
  ).getResultList();
}

@Transactional(readOnly = true)
public Person loadPerson(int id) {
  return this.em.find(Person.class, id);
}

@Transactional
public void savePerson(Person person){
  this.em.persist(person);
}
}
```

This class can perform basic CRUD tasks: finding single or multiple instances of the class as well as saving, updating, or deleting an instance. You'll notice that the SELECT clause looks like it was written in SQL, but it wasn't. JPAQL, JPA's object-oriented query language, is specifically geared toward querying for JPA entity objects rather than tables. There are quite a few things happening in this class:

- PersonServiceImpl: Notice that PersonServiceImpl implements an interface. That's standard practice for DAOs, so that the user of the service doesn't have to know about the guts of the implementation. I'll leave the implementation details of the interface as a practice point.

- @Repository: This Spring annotation has a dual purpose. One, it tells Spring that this class can be imported via classpath scanning. Two, it's a marker for Spring to know that this class requires DAO-specific

`RuntimeException` handling. Using this specific annotation also allows you to quickly group all DAOs through integrated development environment (IDE) searching and lets a reader know at a glance that this class is a DAO.

- `@Transactional`: This annotation lets Spring know that this class requires transaction management, as well as the details as to which types of operations are being performed within each method.

Tip   You can add `@Transactional` at the class level, and doing so will tell Spring that each and every method requires a transaction.

- `EntityManager`: This class is the mechanism for interacting with JPA. It performs CRUD operations in a transaction-aware manner.

Note   By default, all Spring objects are singletons. `EntityManager` is no different, but it is still thread safe and knows about transactional boundaries. Spring passes in a shared proxied `EntityManager`, which delegates to a thread-bound instance of the `EntityManager` that knows all about the context of the request (including transaction boundaries).

- `@PersistenceContext`: This annotation tells Spring that it needs to inject the proxied `EntityMananager`. `@PersistenceContext` can be used on member variables, as shown in the sample, but the preferred approach is to use it on a setter.

Configuring JPA and Spring

We need to fit in a few more pieces of the puzzle before we have a fully working system:

- Create a JPA environment that knows about our `Person` entity.

- Configure Spring with a database connection, a JPA `EntityManager` factory, transaction management and component scanning.

- After setting up all of that, we can move on to actually seeing the DAO in action, through a Springy unit test.

Configuring Our JPA Environment

JPA requires you to create a `META-INF/persistence.xml` file. We're going to create the easiest possible configuration:

```
<persistence
 xmlns="http://java.sun.com/xml/ns/persistence"
 xmlns:xsi="http://www.w3.org/2001/XMLSchema-instance"
 xsi:schemaLocation = "
    http://java.sun.com/xml/ns/persistence
    http://java.sun.com/xml/ns/persistence/ ↪
persistence_1_0.xsd
    "
    version="1.0">
  <persistence-unit name="ArtworkGallery"
    transaction-type="RESOURCE_LOCAL"/>
</persistence>
```

This creates a persistence unit called `ArtworkGallery`. By default, all classes marked as `@Entity` are going to be added to this persistence unit. You can optionally configure which classes you want to include for a given unit, but you generally need to do that only for scenarios more complicated than ours. All you need to do for those scenarios is add `<class>` elements, for example:

```
<persistence
 xmlns="http://java.sun.com/xml/ns/persistence"
 xmlns:xsi="http://www.w3.org/2001/XMLSchema-instance"
 xsi:schemaLocation = "
  http://java.sun.com/xml/ns/persistence
  http://java.sun.com/xml/ns/persistence/ ↪
```

```
persistence_1_0.xsd"
  version="1.0">
    <persistence-unit name="ArtworkGallery"
      transaction-type="RESOURCE_LOCAL">
      <class>com.smartpants.artwork.domain.Person</class>
    </persistence-unit>
</persistence>
```

This configuration is slightly more detailed than what you'll need for the simplest possible JPA configuration, but listing out your entity classes in `persistence.xml` will allow you to see all of your entities in a single location and will reduce startup time, since the list obviates JPA from performing classpath scanning.

JPA is an extremely configurable environment and allows you to set up your environment in quite a few ways, other than what you've seen here. For example, JPA does have a way to set up your system with XML and no annotations whatsoever. Those XML files are an advanced topic that this book can't cover, but they're worth reading up on in other venues.

We now have a basic JPA configuration in place. The Spring environment needs to know how to reference to our `persistences.xml`. Let's explore how we can do that.

Configuring Connections, JPA, Transactions and DAOs in Spring

To perform JPA CRUD operations in Spring, we need a way to create a `EntityMager`. In typical Spring fashion, there's more than one way to configure JPA. We will use a set of JPA `FactoryBeans` similar to the Hibernate-specific `SessionFactoryBean` set of classes.

We're going to use the `LocalContainerEntityManagerFactoryBean` for creating an `EntityMager` that relies purely on Spring configuration for most of what it needs (such as `DataSources`) `LocalContainerEntityManagerFactoryBean`, requires a bit more Spring configuration than other options, but it also gives you more of the

Spring capabilities you learned about in the previous chapters. Setting up a `LocalContainerEntityManagerFactoryBean` requires you to set up a `DataSource` and JPA vendor-specific adapters so that the generic Spring JPA configuration can set up some of the extras required for each vendor.

We're going to use some of the generic Spring configuration we touched on earlier, including the `p-namespace` that reduces the verbosity of setting properties. We're also going to be using context scanning to tell Spring to automatically create DAOs found in specific packages.

Let's create a file called `dataModel.xml` that has the `LocalContainerEntityManagerFactoryBean`, the datasource, a JPA transaction manager and DAO component scanning. We'll start that file off with the namespace setup for the Spring file, and we'll add a whole bunch of Spring namespaces that we'll use to configure JPA:

```
<beans
   xmlns="http://www.springframework.org/schema/beans"
   xmlns:xsi="http://www.w3.org/2001/XMLSchema-instance"
   xmlns:context =
"http://www.springframework.org/schema/context"
   xmlns:tx = "http://www.springframework.org/schema/tx"
   xmlns:p = "http://www.springframework.org/schema/p"
   xsi:schemaLocation="
   http://www.springframework.org/schema/beans
   http://www.springframework.org/schema/beans/ ↵
spring-beans-2.5.xsd
   http://www.springframework.org/schema/context
   http://www.springframework.org/schema/context/ ↵
spring-context-2.5.xsd
   http://www.springframework.org/schema/tx
   http://www.springframework.org/schema/tx/ ↵
spring-tx-2.5.xsd">

   <!-- The rest of the configuration goes here! -->
</beans>
```

You've seen this type of setup before, in Chapter 3. This tells the XML parser that we want to use the following schemas as part of our configuration:

- The default Spring `bean` schema
- The `context` schema for bean scanning and annotation processing
- The `p` schema for easier property settings
- The `tx` schema for transaction management

Next, let's set up an in-memory HSQLDB database datasource:

```
<!-- Local DataSource that
            works in any environment -->
<bean id="dataSource" class=
"org.springframework.jdbc.datasource. ↪
DriverManagerDataSource"
    p:driverClassName="org.hsqldb.jdbcDriver"
    p:url="jdbc:hsqldb:mem:artwork"
    p:username="sa"
    p:password="password"/>
```

You obviously don't have to use an in-memory database; as previously explained, there are plenty of additional ways of getting a datasource, including JNDI lookups and connection pooling.

The `p` namespaces used in the preceding code is yet another option for configuring Spring values. Using `p:url` has the same effect as using the `<property name="url" value=". . .">` XML fragment. You can also use the `p` namespace to create references, as you'll see in the following JPA setup:

```
<!--
    This automatically look for persistence.xml in
    The META-INF directory
-->
<bean id="entityManagerFactory" class=
    "org.springframework.orm.jpa. ↪
```

```
LocalContainerEntityManagerFactoryBean"
    p:dataSource-ref="dataSource">
    <property name="jpaVendorAdapter">
      <bean class=
      "org.springframework.orm.jpa.vendor. ↪
HibernateJpaVendorAdapter"
        p:showSql="true" p:generateDdl="true"
        p:databasePlatform =
          "org.hibernate.dialect.HSQLDialect" />
    </property>
  </bean>
```

As discussed earlier, `LocalContainerEntityManagerFactory` creates a JPA `EntityManager` that is completely Spring-managed. Its `LocalContainerEntityManagerFactory` can use a Spring-managed datasource and a few Hibernate-specific properties (`showSql`, `generateDdl`, and `databasePlatform`).

Note If you want to set other JPA vendor properties, for example, a Hibernate cache provider, you can set them in `persistence.xml`. If that doesn't work for you, you can extend your specific vendor's `JpaVendorAdapter` and override the `getJpaPropertyMap()` method to include a Spring configured `Map` of properties.

Spring provides another `EntityManagerFactoryBean`, `LocalEntityManagerFactoryBean`, and it requires the JPA provider (for example, Hibernate or Eclipse Link) to set up everything it needs, including database connections and a provider-specific load-time weaving setup. The `persistence.xml` file won't be covered here, but the Spring bean would look something like this:

```
<bean id="entityManagerFactory" class=
  "org.springframework.orm.jpa. ↪
LocalEntityManagerFactoryBean">
```

```
  <property name="persistenceUnitName"
    value="ArtworkGallery"/>
</bean>
```

If you're already using a Java EE 6 container, and you want to use EJB3.0, you can use Spring's built in `jndi-lookup` capabilities:

```
<jee:jndi-lookup jndi-lookup id="entityManagerFactory"
    jndi-name="persistence/ArtworkGallery"/>
```

The Spring configuration also needs to include the `<context:annotation-config />` directive. It tells Spring to process all of the JEE annotations, including `@PersistenceContext` that you saw earlier, which will ensure that the correct instance of `EntityManager` will be instantiated and injected into the DAO.

Transaction management in a JPA environment is pretty similar to the one you saw in Chapter 3, with the `HibernateTransactionManager`:

```
<bean id="transactionManager" class =
"org.springframework.orm.jpa.JpaTransactionManager"
    p:dataSource-ref="dataSource"
    p:entityManagerFactory-ref="entityManagerFactory" />

<tx:annotation-driven />
```

The preceding configuration fragment tells Spring to use a JPA transaction manager and that it needs to process `@Transactional` annotations.

The following configuration tells Spring to scan for Java objects that are tagged with the `@Repository` annotation in the `com.smartpants.artwork.dao.jpa` package:

```
<!-- Read in DAOs from the JPA package -->
<context:component-scan base-package=
    "com.smartpants.artwork.dao.jpa"
    use-default-filters="false" >
  <context:include-filter type="annotation"
    expression =
```

```
  "org.springframework.stereotype.Repository" />
    </context:component-scan>
```

The total configuration for creating a database connection, configuring an `EntityManager`, transaction management, and component scanning will look like this:

```
<beans
   xmlns="http://www.springframework.org/schema/beans"
   xmlns:xsi="http://www.w3.org/2001/XMLSchema-instance"
   xmlns:context =
"http://www.springframework.org/schema/context"
   xmlns:tx = "http://www.springframework.org/schema/tx"
   xmlns:p = "http://www.springframework.org/schema/p"
   xsi:schemaLocation="
   http://www.springframework.org/schema/beans
   http://www.springframework.org/schema/beans/ ↪
spring-beans-2.5.xsd
   http://www.springframework.org/schema/context
   http://www.springframework.org/schema/context/ ↪
spring-context-2.5.xsd
   http://www.springframework.org/schema/tx
   http://www.springframework.org/schema/tx/ ↪
spring-tx-2.5.xsd">

   <!-- Local DataSource
             works in any environment -->
   <bean id="dataSource" class=
"org.springframework.jdbc.datasource. ↪
DriverManagerDataSource"
     p:driverClassName="org.hsqldb.jdbcDriver"
     p:url="jdbc:hsqldb:mem:artwork"
     p:username="sa"
     p:password="password"/>

   <!--
     This automatically look for persistence.xml in
     The META-INF directory
```

```
        -->
        <bean id="entityManagerFactory" class=
          "org.springframework.orm.jpa. ↪
LocalContainerEntityManagerFactoryBean"
          p:dataSource-ref="dataSource">
          <property name="jpaVendorAdapter">
            <bean class=
            "org.springframework.orm.jpa.vendor. ↪
HibernateJpaVendorAdapter"
              p:showSql="true" p:generateDdl="true"
              p:databasePlatform =
                "org.hibernate.dialect.HSQLDialect" />
          </property>
        </bean>

        <context:annotation-config />

        <bean id="transactionManager" class =
        "org.springframework.orm.jpa.JpaTransactionManager"
          p:dataSource-ref="dataSource"
          p:entityManagerFactory-ref="entityManagerFactory" />

        <tx:annotation-driven />

        <!-- Read in DAOs from the JPA package -->
        <context:component-scan base-package=
            "com.smartpants.artwork.dao.jpa"
            use-default-filters="false" >
          <context:include-filter type="annotation"
            expression =
        "org.springframework.stereotype.Repository" />
        </context:component-scan>
      </beans>
```

Now that we completed the Spring configuration, let's see the configuration and code in action using a JUnit test!

Unit Testing JPA and Spring

We're going to be testing JPA and Spring with JUnit 4. Spring updated its unit testing environment to be even easier than earlier releases with the addition of well-placed annotations.

```java
@RunWith(SpringJUnit4ClassRunner.class)
@ContextConfiguration(locations =
   {"classpath:dataModel.xml" })
@TransactionConfiguration(
  transactionManager = "transactionManager",
  defaultRollback = true)
@Transactional
public class DomainModelTest {
  @Autowired PersonDao personDao;

  @Test
  public void testPerson() {
    Person person = new Person();
    person.setFirstName("Paul");
    person.setLastName("Fisher");
    person.setUsername("pfisher");
    person.setPassword("password");
        person.setVersion(1);
    personDao.savePerson(person);

    final List<Person> people = personDao.getPeople();
    Assert.assertEquals(1, people.size());
  }
}
```

Spring manages the entire life cycle of the test, including setting dependencies expressed via the `@Autowired` annotation and performing transaction rollback, using the `@Transactional` annotation and the testing-specific `@TransactionConfiguration` annotation. You'll learn about database transactional testing with Spring in Chapter 6, but for now, you can use this test as a running start for a fully functioning JPA application.

Summary

We covered quite a bit about setting up a JPA application in Spring environment in this chapter. You're now armed with enough information to get an end-to-end JPA application working. However, we only touched the surface of what's possible with JPA. The JPA specification includes more annotations. Hibernate has quite a few extensions (some of which we covered in Chapter 3). There are also quite a few vendors besides Hibernate. There's also much more to `EntityManager`, vendor-specific caching solutions, advanced configuration options using `persistence.xml`, and interactions with container-managed JPA (including EJB)! You won't find all those advanced topics in this book, but now you're on your way to understanding them as you need them.

In the next chapter, you'll learn about iBATIS, a lighter-weight framework for database persistence: JPA is an abstraction layer on top of another ORM framework, but iBATIS stays closer to the database layer and provides a simple mapping layer over plain old SQL, while still providing powerful features such as lazy loading and caching.

Chapter 5: Introducing the iBATIS Data Mapper

iBATIS Data Mapper (which includes SQL Map) is an open source persistence framework that provides simple yet powerful abstractions over JDBC. These are roughly analogous to Spring's JDBC abstractions, but iBATIS does provide some additional features. iBATIS configuration includes SQL and straightforward mapping mechanisms to Java objects. iBATIS is a data mapper that maps SQL statements to Java objects; it is not an object-relational mapper (like Hibernate, which maps object metadata such as classes and properties to database metadata such as tables and columns). iBATIS's major differentiator is that you have complete control over the SQL used to interact with your database.

The fact that iBATIS uses SQL as its foundation will work well for legacy systems, and the framework can be learned pretty quickly by a developer who has a SQL background. Here are some additional advantages to using iBATIS:

- iBATIS is easy to learn.
- iBATIS queries are extremely efficient and are just as fast (if not faster) than individual Hibernate queries.
- It provides easy transition from JDBC-centric applications by using preexisting SQL code.
- iBATIS puts SQL in an XML file, which is more string friendly than Java, and then refers to those queries by logical name in Java. This technique is called *using named queries*.

Getting to Know iBATIS

iBATIS is an open-source project started by Clinton Begin in 2001. Begin had a few products, but none of them gained much recognition until the

.NET Pet Shop was released, claiming that .NET was superior to Java in developer productivity and performance.

Microsoft published a paper claiming that .NET's version of Sun's PetStore was ten times faster and four times more productive. Knowing this wasn't the case, Begin responded with a Java-based JPetStore 1.0 in July 2002. Not only did this application have fewer lines of code and a better design than its .NET counterpart but it was implemented by Begin over a few weeks in his spare time!

Begin's goal while writing JPetStore was to prove the benefits of good design, code quality, and productivity. The original .NET Pet Shop had a horrible design with much of the business logic contained in stored procedures, whereas JPetStore had a clean and efficient persistence framework. The JPetStore persistence framework quickly drew the attention of the open source community and grew into the iBATIS framework. The iBATIS framework consists of a DAO framework and SQL Map, an XML-based configuration for managing SQL. Spring has its own DAO framework, but it does support iBATIS SQL Map by providing helper classes to easily configure and use them. Furthermore, the Spring project includes JPetStore as one of its sample applications and has rewritten the JPetStore DAOs to use Spring features.

iBATIS's is released under the Apache License, which means you can use it freely as long as your end-user documentation states that your product contains software developed by the Apache Software Foundation. You can modify the code, but if you do, you can no longer distribute it under the Apache name without permission.

iBATIS is an excellent persistence framework to use with existing or legacy databases. You can easily migrate a JDBC-based application to iBATIS (most of the work involves extracting the SQL out of Java classes and putting it into Java files). Not only is iBATIS fast and efficient but it doesn't hide SQL, which is one of the most powerful and oldest languages in use today. Using iBATIS's SQL Map, developers write SQL in XML files and populate objects based on the results of those queries. Much like the Spring/Hibernate combination, iBATIS DAOs require very few lines of code in each method.

iBATIS now has implementations in Ruby and .NET and is used in MySpace, AbeBooks, and quite a few other projects.

Getting Started with iBATIS

Using Spring and iBATIS consists of a few steps:

1. Setting up SQL Map XML for a specific domain object

2. Writing your Java DAO

3. Configuring the Spring XML for your DAOs and reference SQL Map master list

4. Configuring the SQL Map master list

Setting Up the SQL Map File

We're going to use iBATIS to build the same `Gallery` object that we built in Chapter 2. We'll start out with XML files that contain SQL statements to map a query's inputs and outputs to objects. For the sake of simplicity, we'll call this file `gallerySql.xml`:

```xml
<?xml version="1.0" encoding="UTF-8"?>
<!DOCTYPE sqlMap PUBLIC
    "-//iBATIS.com//DTD SQL Map 2.0//EN"
    "http://www.ibatis.com/dtd/sql-map-2.dtd">
<sqlMap namespace="GallerySQL">
  <insert id="addGallery"
    parameterClass="com.dialmercury.apress.Gallery">
    insert into gallery (id, gallery_name, date)
    values (#id#, #galleryName#, #date#);
    <selectKey resultClass="java.lang.Long"
       keyProperty="id">
```

```xml
        select last_insert_id();
      </selectKey>
   </insert>

   <update id="updateGallery"
        parameterClass="com.dialmercury.apress.Gallery">
     update gallery
     set gallery_name = #galleryName#,
         date = #date#
     where id = #id#;
   </update>

   <select id="getGalleryById"
        parameterClass="java.lang.Long"
        resultClass="com.dialmercury.apress.Gallery">
     select id, gallery_name as galleryName, date
     from gallery
     where id=#id#;
   </select>

   <select id="getGalleriesByDate"
        parameterClass="java.util.Date"
        resultClass="com.dialmercury.apress.Gallery">
     select id, gallery_name as galleryName, date
     from gallery
     where date=#date#;
   </select>

   <delete id="deleteGallery"
     parameterClass="java.lang.Long">
     delete from gallery
     where id = #id#;
   </delete>
 </sqlMap>
```

It's easy to spot the familiar insert, update, delete, and select SQL statements in the XML. These example statements are very simple and easy to understand, and more complex SQL and stored procedures can be used just as simply.

Note that each statement can optionally specify a `parameterClass` or `resultClass` attribute. There are simple uses of `parameterClass`, such as `getGalleriesByDate` and `deleteGallery`, that use a single parameter (`Date` and `Long` respectively). If you need more parameters, you need to put them all in a POJO and use the properties of the POJO to the dynamic values found in the query. For example, `addGallery` and `updateGallery` have a `paramaterClass` of `Gallery`; `#id#` translates to `gallery.getId()`; and `#galleryName#` translates to `gallery.getGalleryName()`. Also, `getGalleriesByDate()` uses `Gallery` as a `resultClass` and translates each row in the SQL results into a `Gallery` instance, with `#id#` being set by `gallery.setId()` and `#galleryName#` being set by `gallery.setGalleryName()`.

Writing the DAO

Spring provides a convenience wrapper around iBATIS SQL Maps. `SqlMapClientDaoSupport`. `SqlMapClientDaoSupport` wraps iBATIS's `SqlMapClient`, as shown in the following example:

```
package com.dialmercury.apress;

//use your IDE to organize imports
public class IBatisJdbcImageGalleryDao
extends SqlMapClientDaoSupport
implements ImageGalleryDao {

  public Gellery getImageGalleryById(Long id) {
    return (Gallery) getSqlMapClientTemplate()
      .queryForObject("getGalleryById", id);
  }

  public List<ImageGallery> getImageGalleryByDate(
    Date date) {
```

```java
    return new ArrayList<ImageGallery>(
      getSqlMapClientTemplate().queryForList(
        "getGalleryByDate",date)
      .toArray(new Gallery[0]);
  }

  public void saveImageGallery(ImageGallery gallery) {
    if (gallery.getId() == null) {
      // Use iBATIS's <selectKey> feature,
      // which is db-specific
      Long id = (Long) getSqlMapClientTemplate()
        .insert("addGallery", gallery);
      gallery.setId(id);
    } else {
      getSqlMapClientTemplate()
        .update("updateGallery", user);
    }
  }

  // for completeness
  public void removeGallery(Long id) {
    getSqlMapClientTemplate().update(
      "deleteGallery", id);
  }
}
```

Configuring Spring

Of course, Spring has to be told how to use iBATIS, and it needs a database connection:

```xml
<?xml version="1.0" encoding="UTF-8"?>
<!DOCTYPE beans PUBLIC "-//SPRING//DTD BEAN//EN"
"http://www.springframework.org/dtd/spring-beans.dtd">

<beans>

  <!-- This is the same data source definition
```

```
        as
  chapter 2 -->
   <bean id="dataSource"
     class="org.springframework.jdbc. ↵
datasource.DriverManagerDataSource">
     <property name="driverClassName" value=
         "com.hsqldb.jdbcDriver" />
     <property name="url" value=
         "jdbc:mysql://localhost/imagegalleryt " />
     <property name="username" value="blah" />
     <property name="password" value="1234" />
   </bean>

   <!-- Configure IBatis -->
   <bean id="sqlMapClient"
    class="org.springframework.orm. ↵
ibatis.SqlMapClientFactoryBean">
     <property name="configLocation">
       value="classpath:/sql-map-config.xml" />
     <property name="dataSource" ref="dataSource" />
   </bean>

   <!-- Configure the DAO -->
   <bean id="imageGalleryDao"
     class="com.dialmercury.apress. ↵
IBatisJdbcImageGalleryDao">
     <property name="sqlMapClient" ref="sqlMapClient" />
   </bean>

</beans>
```

Did you notice the `sql-map-config.xml` path? That's the iBATIS
configuration file, which includes the SQL statements and iBATIS object
mapping. It can really be called anything you'd like, but `sql-map-config.xml` is pretty common.

Configuring SQL Map

An iBATIS project will likely contain plenty of SQL Map files, one per domain object. All of those SQL Map files must be referenced from a configuration file: this is the `sql-map-config.xml` file defined in the Spring configuration file.

```xml
<?xml version="1.0" encoding="UTF-8"?>
<!DOCTYPE sqlMapConfig PUBLIC
"-//iBATIS.com//DTD SQL Map Config 2.0//EN"
"http://www.ibatis.com/dtd/sql-map-config-2.dtd">

<sqlMapConfig>
  <settings enhancementEnabled="true"
    maxTransactions="32" maxRequests="512"
    maxSessions="128" />
  <sqlMap resource="gallerySQL.xml" />
</sqlMapConfig>
```

Here are some handy things to note about the preceding code snippet:

- `enhancementEnabled="true"` tells iBATIS to proxy results to allow optimized JavaBean property access and lazy loading. By default, the value for `enhancementEnabled` is `false`.

- `maxRequests` tells iBATIS the maximum allowed concurrent number of SQL requests that should be executed. The default value is 512.

- `maxTransactions` tells iBATIS the maximum of allowed concurrent transactions. The maximum depends on the specific database you use, but these limits do exist. `maxTransactions` should be about a tenth of `maxRequests`. Sometimes, reducing the maximum transactions increases performance.

- `maxSessions` represents the maximum number of concurrent sessions that iBATIS should allow. The value for `maxSessions` should be between `maxRequests` and `maxTransactions`.

- A value of `false` for `cacheModelsEnabled` disables caching. By default, this value is `true`. `cacheModelsEnabled` is handy for debugging.

- A value of false for `lazyLoadingEnabled` disables lazy loading. Like `cacheModelsEnabled`, it's `true` by default, and a value of `false` is handy for debugging.

See iBATIS's documentation for more information on the `<settings>` element; there are actually a few more interesting options that you can use that were not mentioned here.

Moving Beyond the Basics

You should now be able to use iBATIS in your application. You've seen how to configure SQL Map, create a DAO, and use it in Spring. Though using iBATIS really is that simple, the data mapper is far from simplistic. You can definitely do a lot more with iBATIS than just the basics.

Mapping Results

iBATIS provides excellent mapping for simple properties by mapping a column in the result of a select statement to a JavaBean property without much work. iBATIS calls that type of mapping an *implicit mapping*. iBATIS allows you to have a custom mapping from SQL results to single objects, results to objects with nested objects, and even results to plain old `HashMaps`. The results to nested objects can be performed with either a single query with multiple objects returned or two sets of queries with a parent/child relationship.

Here are a couple more versions of select statements that will give you an idea how to use some of the more complicated mappings:

```
<resultMap id="galleryMapping"
    parameterClass="com.dialmercury.apress.Gallery">
  <result property="id" property="ID"
    column_index="1" />
```

```xml
<result property="galleryName"
  property="GALLERY_NAME"
  column_index="2" />
<result property="date" property="DATE"
  column_index="3" />
</resultMap>

<select id="getGalleryById"
  parameterClass="java.lang.Long"
  resultMap="galleryMapping">
  select ID, GALLERY_NAME, DATE
  from gallery
  where ID=#id#;
</select>

<select id="getGalleryByIdAsHashtable"
  parameterClass="java.lang.Long"
  resultClass="java.util.HashMap">
  select ID, GALLERY_NAME, DATE
  from gallery
  where ID=#id#;
</select>
```

Using Dynamic SQL

Hibernate provides a complex feature for generating queries by example.
iBATIS has a similar XML-based feature. This feature allows the same
configuration to be used in multiple scenarios in your application. The
following example, while simple, illustrates some of the capabilities of
iBATIS's dynamic SQL feature:

```xml
<select id="getGallery" resultMap="get-product-result">
  SELECT id, gallery_name as galleryName, date
  FROM GALLERY
  <dynamic prepend="WHERE">
    <isNotNull prepend="and" property="id">
      id = #id#
    </isNotNull>
```

```
        <isNotNull prepend="and" property="date">
          date = #date#
        </isNotNull>
    </dynamic>
  </select>
```

If you pass in no values for id or date, you'll get this:

```
SELECT id, gallery_name as galleryName, date
FROM GALLERY
```

If you pass in an id of 123, getGallery will return this:

```
SELECT id, gallery_name as galleryName, date
FROM GALLERY
WHERE id = 123
```

There are quite a few conditional (if-then) and iterative (looping) XML elements that you can mix and match to produce a wide variety of conditions using a single iBATIS select element.

Caching

iBATIS has a built-in caching module. This mechanism allows you to use either the iBATIS built-in caching mechanism or the OSCache open source caching project. Here's an example configuration for the GallerySQL SQL map:

```
<sqlMap namespace="GallerySQL">
  <cacheModel id="galleryCache" type="LRU">
    <flushInterval hours="24" />
    <flushOnExecute statement="addGallery" />
    <property name="size" value="1000" />
  </cacheModel>

  <select id="getGalleryById"
      parameterClass="java.lang.Long"
      resultClass="com.dialmercury.apress.Gallery"
      cacheModel="galleryCache">
    select id, gallery_name as galleryName, date
```

```
        from gallery
        where id=#id#;
    </select>
      ...
  </sqlMap>
```

In the preceding example, the LRU type stands for *last recently used*, which is one algorithm for determining which objects to remove from the cache once the number of objects in the cache reaches the maximum size. Also, notice the size property, which lets you define the maximum number of objects that you can have in the cache.

The cache processing happens when the getSqlMapClientTemplate(). queryForObject("getGalleryById", id) method is called. iBATIS checks the cache named galleryCache for a cached object based on a unique key that includes the ID. If the object is in the cache, iBATIS returns that object instead of going to the database. That leads to significant performance boosts for your application.

iBATIS is smart enough to know when to clear values in the cache based on your application logic. In our case, if you add a new gallery, iBATIS will clear the cache whenever the updateGallery statement is run. You can add as many flushOnExecute statements as you'd like; for example, you can add another flushOnExecute statement for deleteGallery.

We'll consider another caching alternative that in Chapter 8: the Spring caching module, which is part of the Spring Modules project. It allows you to use a wide variety of open source caching options and is configured through either annotations in your DAO or XML file.

Managing Transactions

Spring does provide out-of-the-box transaction management that will meet your needs. The Spring transaction is declarative, nonintrusive, and comprehensive.

However, it is worth mentioning that iBATIS does provide a programmatic transaction management feature as well.

As we mentioned earlier, Spring provides extensible enterprise features such as declarative transaction management and caching. In addition, Spring maps iBATIS's exception hierarchy to a standard exception hierarchy. Spring also provides complex filesystem configuration options, as well as complex data source management. Spring's DAO wrappers help decouple your service layer from the data retrieval implementation details.

Summary

You can learn to use iBATIS very quickly and write less code than when using traditional JDBC alternatives. iBATIS provides some great advanced features that should satisfy relatively complex projects. Complex legacy databases are iBATIS's sweet spot.

Using iBATIS with Spring will definitely has some great benefits. Spring brings declarative transactions, declarative caching, exception management, and extensive configuration options.

In the next chapter, you'll find out about one of the more enjoyable aspects of database development, ACID transactions. You'll also learn about caching. In other words, you'll be caching in on ACID transactions.

Chapter 6: Managing Transactions

Database transactions help you group a set of operations into a single unit of work. All operations succeed, or fail, as a group. Spring's powerful and flexible transaction support is another factor responsible for the framework's success and popularity. Prior to Spring, complex or declarative transactional features typically required a JEE server. Using Aspect-Oriented-Programming (AOP) techniques, Spring helped democratize enterprise-level transactional support, allowing developers to cleanly apply transactional rules to their code whether they were using a full-fledged JEE application server, a lighter weight web container, or even a stand-alone unit test. The important detail is that the transactional rules could be consolidated into configuration so that code need not be muddied with these types of concerns. Switching between a JEE application server, using a Java Transaction API (JTA) datasource and a simple unit test, and a local datasource is just a matter of modifying the Spring configuration; no code needs to be altered. However, Spring can leverage some of the advanced features offered by JTA when employing a JTA transaction manager. The key benefit, however, is that Spring provides a transactional programming model that is consistent, whether you need to have transactions span multiple datasources (a feature offered by JTA) or across a single datasource, the way in which you define these transactional concerns will always be the same when using Spring.

Spring allows you to control how transactions are performed at a per-method level. Transaction management can be applied via XML configuration or using Java 5 annotations. In this chapter, we will demonstrate both approaches. However, we recommend using annotations, as this strategy is the most intuitive and allows transactional metadata to be embedded directly within a service layer class or interface.

Before pursuing the details of how Spring performs transaction management, it's important to understand some of the fundamental and theoretical concepts. There's quite a bit to know about transactions, but the most important details to understand are encapsulated in the acronym ACID: atomicity, consistency, isolation, and durability. In this chapter, you will learn the fundamentals of ACID transactions, as well as how to declaratively apply transactions using Spring. These concepts will undoubtedly prove useful for any type of application development, and if nothing else, they will come in handy during your next job interview.

Note   We recommend waiting for these topics to come up themselves; in the context of a job interview, we do not recommend starting out by confessing your love for ACID.

The Joy of ACID

Transactions are all about ACID. Transactions delineate general rules for how a database should behave in the context of a unit of work. ACID compliance considers the following key factors:

- *Atomicity*: Either all of your data is saved (or deleted) or none of it is.

- *Consistency*: Your database has a whole bunch of rules, such as referential integrity and constraints. Those rules must apply both before and after the transaction.

- *Isolation*: If you have multiple transactions occurring at the same time, they don't affect one another.

- *Durability*: Once data is committed, it stays committed.

ACID can be perceived as a bit trippy, but it has a way of keeping your data safe and will definitely maintain your sanity when dealing with persistence.

So why should you care about ACID? It's important to understand the available rules and options of database behavior so that you can effectively leverage these features in the context of your application. These details are critical for controlling how a group of operations are applied to a database or how concurrent database modifications can affect each other

Controlling the ACID Problem

In earlier chapters, we covered several examples of how transactional management can be applied to a service layer using Spring. Let's review a bit about what you learned earlier.

Transactions define how and when data is committed to a database; they are indispensable in grouping persistence logic together, ensuring that all methods complete successfully or that the database is rolled back to its previous state. Prior to Spring, this capability was one of the primary benefits to using EJB.

For most operations, you also need to be concerned with transactional details, ensuring that transactions are started at the beginning of an operation and are either committed or rolled back when the operation completes.

Spring enables these features through three core concepts:

- *Platform transaction management* refers to how commits and rollbacks work. Hibernate, iBATIS, and JPA each have their own transaction implementations. Furthermore, transactions typically operate differently in a testing environment than an EJB server. Spring abstracts these details.

- *Declarative transaction management* allows developers to specify the transactional details that should apply to a method through metadata or configuration. Obviously, the code to set up, commit, and rollback a given transaction is still getting executed. However, these details may be separated from the code itself and placed into configuration files or annotations.

- *Programmatic transaction management* explicitly controls the transaction through code. Spring provides a transaction template that can greatly simplify the code required to apply transactional semantics to a given method.

However, this approach requires that transactional details be blended with business logic.

Platform Transaction Management

Spring's `TransactionManager` objects fill the role of (drum roll please): managing transactions. `TransactionManager` instances all extend the `PlatformTransactionManager` class and know how to access or initiate transactions, roll back transactions, and commit transactions. The interface looks like this:

```
public interface PlatformTransactionManager {
  TransactionStatus getTransaction(
    TransactionDefinition definition) throws
    TransactionException;

  void commit(TransactionStatus status) throws
    TransactionException;

  void rollback(TransactionStatus status) throws
    TransactionException;
}
```

There are quite a few `TransactionManager` implementations: The `DataSourceTransactionManager` is used for JDBC and iBATIS implementations. A few of the ORM-based `TransactionManagers` include `HibernateTransactionManager`, `JpaTransactionManager`, `JdoTransactionManager`, and `TopLinkTransactionManager`. You'll even find `TransactionManagers` for the JTA used by EJB. JTA transactions can be set up to span multiple databases and even disparate technologies, such as Java Message Service (JMS). These transaction managers include the generic `JtaTransactionManager` and implementations for specific EJB servers like `OC4JtaTransactionManager` for Oracle's server, `WeblogicJtaTransactionManager` for BEA's server, and

`WebSphereUowTransactionManager` for IBM's server. However, using the `<tx:jta-transaction-manager/>` XML tag within your configuration file will allow Spring to determine which JTA transaction manager to use based on runtime information, so that you don't have to explicitly reference the platform-specific configuration. We'll explore the `tx` namespace a bit later in this chapter.

You might have noticed the `TransactionStatus` and `TransactionDefinition` classes that are part of the `PlatformTransactionManager` interface. You usually don't have to use these `classes` yourself; they are set up by Spring's declarative transaction management (which we'll discuss shortly), but they are still worth knowing about.

`TransactionStatus` encapsulates key information related to an actively running transaction, such as whether or not a new transaction has been created and whether the transaction should be rolled back or committed. It also allows the transaction to be marked as `Rollback-Only`.

The `TransactionDefinition` that you saw in the code for `PlatformTransactionManager` keeps track of the ACID properties we talked about earlier, including things like how your transaction needs to be isolated from other transactions, whether your transaction will perform any writes (or is read-only), and even how long the transaction can run before timing out.

Declarative Transaction Management

Declarative programming is basically describing what you want rather than how you want it done. Using declarative transaction management, therefore, implies that you describe how you want your transactions to behave rather than interspersing transactional behavior in your code. As you've seen earlier, Spring has a fantastic annotation-driven approach for transaction management. However, you have not yet seen an XML-driven strategy based on Spring configuration. We will discuss all of these approaches in more detail throughout this chapter.

It's important to note that Spring's declarative transaction management works at the method level. Later in this chapter, we'll discuss a few implications this can have. We'll also discuss a few scenarios in which refactoring methods to be more transaction-friendly was able to solve some relatively common problems.

Since we've used annotation-based transaction examples in several earlier chapters, let's start with an overview of this approach.

Using @Transactional for ACID Transactional Annotations

Let's go over some of the values you can set on a `@Transactional` annotation that you've seen all over the place in this book (or at least on some `Service` and `DAO` objects):

- *Propagation*: This defines the transactional behavior for the specified method. This setting determines whether a new transaction should always be created, whether a nested transaction should be created, or even if no transaction should be created at all. Here are the propagation values you can use in Spring:

  - `REQUIRED`: If there's a transaction, support it; otherwise, create a new one.

  - `SUPPORTS`: It's OK, whether or not there's a transaction.

  - `MANDATORY`: There must be a transaction; otherwise, throw an exception.

  - `REQUIRES_NEW`: Create a new transaction and suspend the current one if it exists.

  - `NOT_SUPPORTED`: Execute nontransactionally and suspend the current transaction.

  - `NEVER`: Throw an exception if a transaction exists.

- **NESTED**: Perform a nested transaction if a transaction exists; otherwise, create a new transaction. Did you know that you can have a transaction within a transaction? It's a bit mind altering!

- *Isolation*: Isolation is the *I* in ACID and helps to determine how this transaction is affected by other database processes occurring within the application. There are three settings to control isolation behavior for a given transaction:

  - **DEFAULT**: Let the datastore define the isolation level.

  - **READ_UNCOMMITED**: Dirty, dirty reads—ACID isn't a consideration, because consistency isn't an issue. This isolation level

  - **READ_COMMITTED**: Dirty and nonrepeatable reads are not allowed, but phantom reads are. Only data that has been committed is accessible.

- **readOnly**: This specifies whether this transaction is read-only. A `readOnly` value of `true` ensures that the method only performs read operations.

- **timeout**: This setting defines how long a transaction can live without committing or rolling back.

- **rollbackFor/rollbackForClassName**: This setting allows you to specify an array of either classes or class names (depending on the setting used) of exceptions that, when thrown, will trigger an automatic rollback of the currently executing transaction. For example, if we specified the class `InvalidImageException` for a service method intended to save an `ArtEntity` domain class, a transaction would be rolled back should that exception ever be thrown.

- **noRollbackForClass/noRollbackForClassName**: This one works the same way as the preceding setting but prevents a transaction from being rolled back should one of the specified exception classes get thrown while this transaction is being executed.

XML-Driven Transaction Configuration

Now that you have a better understanding of the capabilities built into the
`@Transactional` annotation, you now need to learn how to actually get
these annotations to do their jobs. Annotations by themselves are not
inherently useful; we need some other mechanism to apply meaning to
these annotations. That's where AOP comes into play. We introduced AOP
in Chapter 1 and demonstrated some XML configuration that enables
Spring to manage transactions via AOP. You've learned how to
declaratively apply transactions in several examples throughout this book.
Let's review a JPA example from Chapter 4:

```
<bean id="transactionManager" class =
"org.springframework.orm.jpa.JpaTransactionManager"
    p:dataSource-ref="dataSource"
    p:entityManagerFactory-ref="entityManagerFactory" />

    <tx:annotation-driven />
```

This XML snippet instructs Spring to use the `JpaTransactionManager`
and to add an AOP proxy to all objects that Spring manages that contain a
`@Transactional` annotation. Of course, you can swap out the
`JpaTransactionManager` for the `HibernateTransactionManager`,
`DatasourceTransactionManager`, or one of the JTA transaction
managers.

tx:annotation-driven

The `tx:annotation-driven` annotation supports the following features:

- `transaction-manager`: This supplies the name of the bean used for the
  transaction manager. Theoretically, you can have more than one transactional
  manager in your spring application context and only use one. The default
  value is `transactionManager`.

- `mode`: This specifies the type of proxying mechanism you want. You have a choice of either `proxy`, to use Spring proxying, or `aspectj` to use AspectJ, an industrial strength AOP framework. The default is `proxy`.

- `proxy-target-class`: By default, Spring creates a Java `Proxy` object, and only attaches the interfaces that the object implements. For example, if you have a `PersonDaoJPA` class that implements a `PersonDao` interface, the proxying process will create an object that implements `PersonDao`, adds on the implementation of your transactional semantics, and passes the request to your implementation. If the class doesn't implement any interfaces or you need the proxy to extend the class and not just its interfaces, Spring will use the CGLib open source byte code manipulation framework to perform the proxying. The CGLib approach does have a limitation: you have to put the transactional annotations on the class itself and not on the interface.

- `order`: Plenty of other frameworks take advantage of proxying, but to use them, you may have to explicitly order the transactional and other proxying mechanisms. Lower order numbers get processed first.

tx:advice

So far, we've spoken only about the `@Transactional` annotation for applying transactional semantics. You can also use a pure-XML–driven approach, which is helpful for cases where you either don't want to apply annotations or can't because you need to use JDK1.4 or want to apply transactional semantics to a library that you can't change. Coupling the `tx:advice` XML configuration with an XML-based AOP configuration makes for a pretty powerful combination. For example, you can use method names to automatically figure out what kind of transactionality you want to apply.

Here's an example specifying that methods starting with *save*, *update*, and *delete* require a transaction, and everything else supports (but does not require) a read-only transaction:

```
<tx:advice id="txAdvice" >
  <tx:attributes>
    <tx:method name="save*" propagation="REQUIRED"/>
    <tx:method name="update*" propagation="REQUIRED"/>
    <tx:method name="delete*" propagation="REQUIRED"/>
    <tx:method name="*" propagation="SUPPORTS"
      read-only="true"/>
  </tx:attributes>
</tx:advice>
```

tx:advice does support a transaction-manager XML attribute, but by default, it uses the name transactionManager, just like tx:annotation-driven.

In addition to the flexible method name matching, the tx:method element has the same types of parameters as the @Transactional annotation. You can set values for propogation, isolation, timeout, read-only, rollback-for, and no-rollback-for. All of those tx:method XML attributes have the same values as their @Transactional counterparts.

One more detail needs to be added to this example in order to make it complete. We need to use Spring's AOP framework to define which beans need the advice. We can accomplish this by using the aop namespace in our Spring XML file. For example, if we wanted to apply the transactional advice to all of the classes that are in the com.smartpants.artwork.service package, we can add the following to our Spring XML file:

```
<aop:config>
  <aop:pointcut id="allServices"
    expression = "execution(*  ↪
com.smartpants.artwork.service.*.*(..))"/>
  <aop:advisor advice-ref="txAdvice"
    pointcut-ref="allServices"/>
</aop:config>
```

Spring AOP is pretty flexible and even lets you use annotations to define the pointcut. If we want to apply the `txAdvice` to any class that is annotated with `@Transactional`, we can change the `allServices` pointcut to this:

```
<aop:pointcut id="allServices" expression=
"@target(org.springframework.transaction.annotation ↪
.Transactional)"/>
```

We can even combine the two pointcut approaches like so:

```
<aop:pointcut id="allServices" expression=
"execution(* com.smartpants.artwork.service. ↪
*.*(..)) && @target(org.springframework. ↪
transaction.annotation.Transactional)"/>
```

Let's take a look at one more Spring AOP trick—using the bean name to define a pointcut. If we want to apply our transaction to a bean named `personService`, we can do the following:

```
<aop:pointcut id="allServices"
    expression ="bean(personService)"/>
```

We can also use the asterisk (*) wildcard character to match against all beans that end with `Service` or `Dao` as follows:

```
<aop:pointcut id="allServices"
  expression ="bean(*Service) || bean(*Dao)"/>
```

If applying complex AOP pointcuts to ACID transactions is still a bit too mind-altering for you, you'll find plenty of documentation out there. However, the information you've gleaned here should give you a running start in understanding how to get your ACID transactions in order.

Examining Transactional Examples

Before we move on to the next topic, let's go through a couple of real-world scenarios so that you gain an even better understanding of some of the concepts we discussed in the last section.

Creating a Batch Application

Batch applications can be a bit of a drag, especially with Object Relational Mappers (ORMs). Both the database and the ORM need to reserve valuable resources for each operation performed in a transaction. The database needs to keep locks on the tables that we've changed. The ORM, for a variety of reasons, needs to cache the objects that we've persisted and read from the database. The more operations a transaction executes, the more resources the ORM and database need to dedicate to our transaction. Let's start out with the following example, which updates a whole bunch of records:

```
@Transactional(readOnly = false,
   propagation = Propagation.SUPPORTS)
public void batchProcessAll() {
   int count = dao.getCount();
   // do your ACID business in a big for loop
}
```

We may be able to find smaller units that can be committed, which will free up some of the resources utilized by the database and ORM framework. However, the process of committing the transaction consumes resources as well. If we commit too often, we'll probably decrease performance. There's a balance between committing too often and too little, for example, committing after a certain number of items have been processed. We can create a method that processes x number of units and commits after it completes. It's actually quite simple to set this up. We'll choose 100 as an arbitrary number of units of work:

```
// no transaction on this method anymore
public void batchProcessAll() {
   int count = dao.getCount();
   for(int i=0; i<count; i+= 100){
      doMyUnit(i, i+100);
   }
}
```

```
@Transactional(readOnly = false,
   propagation = Propagation.REQUIRES_NEW)
public void doMyUnit(int start, int finish) {
   // do your ACID business from the unit's
   // start to finish
   dao.flush();
}
```

Note the use of `Propagation.REQUIRES_NEW`. It tells Spring that a new transaction begins when the method gets invoked and commits when the method completes. It's just that simple to create and commit a transaction.

Using Two Datasources

Assume you have two databases, and you want to apply the right transactions to the right beans. You have to create two different `transactionManagers` that need to be applied to the appropriate subsets of Spring beans. You can do that with some fancy AOP work. Assume that you have already configured `transactionManager1` and `transactionManager2` beans. You'll need to start with the following XML:

```
<tx:advice id="txAdvice1"
   transaction-manager="transaction-manager1" >
   <tx:attributes>
     <tx:method name="save*" propagation="REQUIRED"/>
     <tx:method name="update*" propagation="REQUIRED"/>
     <tx:method name="delete*" propagation="REQUIRED"/>
     <tx:method name="*" propagation="SUPPORTS"
        read-only="true"/>
   </tx:attributes>
</tx:advice>

<tx:advice id="txAdvice2"
    transaction-manager="transaction-manager2" >
   <tx:attributes>
```

```
      <tx:method name="save*" propagation="REQUIRED"/>
      <tx:method name="update*" propagation="REQUIRED"/>
      <tx:method name="delete*" propagation="REQUIRED"/>
      <tx:method name="*" propagation="SUPPORTS"
        read-only="true"/>
    </tx:attributes>
  </tx:advice>

  <aop:config>
    <aop:advisor advice-ref="txAdvice1"
      pointcut-ref="allDatabaseOneBeans"/>
    <aop:advisor advice-ref="txAdvice2"
      pointcut-ref="allDatabaseTwoBeans"/>
    <!-- Add pointcuts here -->
  </aop:config>
```

The `tx:advice` element tells Spring *what* needs to be done, and the `aop:config` element tells Spring *where* it needs to be done.

The question now is what beans should have which advice? Some beans need `txAdvice1`; others need `txAdvice2`; and others may need both. Thankfully, Spring AOP provides us with myriad mapping options: We can organize our classes into packages that differentiate between the two datasources to which they relate and apply an expression pointcut. Or we can devise logical bean names that clearly infer which advice to apply. We can also create our own annotations, `@Transaction1` and `@Transaction2`, for example, and use the `expression="@target(...)"` approach.

Let's go through a quick bean name example. Imagine we have two datasources: `datasource1` and `datasource2`. Let's say that each of the `datasource1` beans has `ds1` as part of its bean name. For example, if `PersonDao` is intended to interface with `datasource1`, it would be called `ds1.personDao`. If `PersonService` depends on `personDao` as well as a DAO from `datasource2`, it should be called `ds1.ds2.personService`. Our pointcuts will look like the following:

```
<aop:pointcut id="allDatabaseOneBeans"
   expression ="bean(*ds1*)"/>
<aop:pointcut id="allDatabaseTwoBeans"
   expression ="bean(*ds2*)"/>
```

In the preceding example, we've defined two pointcut expressions that utilize a bean-naming convention to properly infer which datasource and `transactionManager` to utilize for a given transaction.

Summary

In this chapter, you've learned both the fundamentals and low-level details for managing database transactions with Spring. We've explored two different avenues for applying transactions declaratively with Spring: via annotation and through XML-based Spring configuration. It's also possible to utilize Spring's transaction management programmatically, through the use of the transaction template. However this approach couples transactional behavior with the application's business logic.

Understanding how transactions work, along with the available configuration options, is critical for developing and debugging multiuser applications. We've discussed both simple and complex scenarios in this chapter, and we hope they give you a taste of what's possible when using Spring for transaction management.

Most important, Spring provides a consistent approach for applying transactional semantics to an application—no matter what the architecture or environment. This means that you can configure and code your application the same way, regardless of whether you're deploying to a JEE application server using a JTA datasource or a lightweight container with a local datasource. The difference is just a matter of configuration.

Next, you'll learn about testing the persistence tier of our application using Spring and JUnit.

Chapter 7: Integration Testing with JUnit

Automated testing has been a hot topic for quite a while, almost to the point of being a de facto requirement for projects. JUnit is the most popular implementation of automated testing frameworks, and Spring integrates with it quite well. You'll find other automated testing frameworks out there, but we'll stick with the ubiquitous JUnit (specifically JUnit 4.4) and Spring integration to perform common automated testing needs.

Testing is one of Spring's strong suits. First and foremost, testing is among the best practices that Spring encourages; other best practices include layering and coding to interfaces, which you saw earlier. A code base that is broken down into layers such that each layer has a unique responsibility is much more testable than code that does a whole bunch of stuff in one location. Testable code is code that you can easily test, and well-layered code is testable because it produces small, defined parts of the overall picture. The fact that you've coded to interfaces and using dependency injection allows you to stub (or mock) one layer (such as the DAO layer) when you're testing the layer above it (in this case, the service layer that uses DAOs). The setters and getters in your code base make it completely decoupled from the Spring dependency injection engine, and therefore, you can test your code outside of Spring.

In addition, you can use Spring dependency injection to separate the logic from the configuration of your tests, or you can even use tests to confirm that your Spring `ApplicationContext` is configured properly.

Integration Testing

With Spring, you can run your testing outside of a server. You can switch between different database implementations and datasources. You can split your application into smaller modules and test each component separately.

Unit testing is very effective at verifying that a particular class works properly in isolation. Seeing classes in isolation is very valuable, and there is no effective replacement for a good unit test. However, integration tests are useful too, as they are most effective at replicating the way in which your code will behave within an actual production environment.

Unlike unit testing, *integration testing* typically verifies multiple components simultaneously. For instance, a common practice is to instantiate the Spring `ApplicationContext` and test a DAO implementation using a real, live database along with the Spring ORM or JDBC template abstractions. The advantage of this approach is that you are touching multiple components, ensuring that all the pieces are working together properly. The disadvantage is that it doesn't provide much granularity to ascertain whether a particular component is working properly.

Using JUnit 4.4 and Annotations to Facilitate Testing

Let's take a look at JUnit before we get into too much Spring-specific testing.

JUnit 4.4's approach is highly annotation based. The `@Test` annotation is all you need to add to create a test:

```
public class SimpleTest{
  @Test
  public void testSimpleStuff(){
    String name = "Paul";
    Assert.assertEquals("Paul", name);
  }
}
```

A couple of additional basic JUnit annotations can help with the life cycle of the test. You can run some code right before and after each test using `@Before` and `@After`. Guess which one comes before a test? You can also run code before and after all tests in a particular class using `@BeforeClass` and `@AfterClass`. There's also an `@Ignore` annotation, which allows you to use an `@Test` annotation and not run a particular method!

```java
public class SimpleTest{
    public static String staticName = null;
    public String memberName = null;

    @BeforeClass
    public static void initializeClass(){
        staticName = "Paul";
    }

    @Before
    public void initializeTest(){
      memberName = "Solomon";
    }

    @Test
    public void testSimpleStuff(){
       Assert.assertEquals("Paul", staticName);
    }

    @Test
    @Ignore public void dontTestThis(){
       // notice that this would fail
       Assert.assertEquals("Paul", memberName);
    }

  }
```

These JUnit annotations are just the tip of the iceberg. One of the more interesting additional annotations is `@RunWith`, which lets you define some additional features to run as part of your tests. Spring takes advantage of `@RunWith` to add some dependency injection and transactional functionality that you'll see in the "Testing with a Database" section of this chapter.

Before we move on to Spring, we'd like to say a quick word about test suites. A *test suite* is a set of individual JUnit test classes. For example, you can create a DAO test suite composed of all of your DAO tests. The following example shows all you need to do to create a suite of tests:

```
public void static testSuite(){
    return new TestSuite(
        ArtworkDao.class, CategoryDao.class,
        ExhibitionDao.class, PersonDao.class);
}
```

Modern IDEs (Eclipse, IntelliJ IDEA, NetBeans and many more) and other runtime environments (such as ANT and Maven) know how to run both individual JUnit tests and test suites.

Spring JUnit 4 Extensions

Spring testing includes a combination of XML, annotations, and dependency injection.

The XML comes into play in a similar fashion to the examples you've seen earlier in this book. Your tests use the same XML code (more or less) that you use in your application. You can override a few small beans, such as your datasource, for your tests and keep all of your application DAOs and service objects.

Quite a few Spring-specific annotations are available to get the test configuration stored in your application and the test XML into a running JUnit test. If you paid attention before, you're probably guessing that we're referring to JUnit's @RunWith annotation. Adding @RunWith(SpringJUnit4ClassRunner.class) to your unit test will tell JUnit that it needs to call Spring for some additional setup steps before your tests can run.

SpringJUnit4ClassRunner looks for some additional annotations to perform its setup. For example, it looks for a @ContextConfiguration annotation that defines the locations of your configuration files. Let's say that, in your application, you have defined a couple of XML files named `dataModel.xml` and `spring-test-datasource.xml`. `dataModel.xml` defines a `PersonDao` and `datasource.xml` defines your datasource. You can import this configuration by adding the following annotation:

```
@ContextConfiguration(locations =
    {"classpath:dataModel.xml",
     "classpath:spring-test-datasource.xml"})
```

Spring configuration is nice, but now, you're probably wondering how you can access some beans that are defined in your configuration. Do you remember the `@Autowired` annotation that Spring-managed beans can use? You can use it in your test code to tell the Spring JUnit Runner that you need some Spring beans. Here's what the `PersonDAO` test code looks like when we put all of this together:

```
@RunWith(SpringJUnit4ClassRunner.class)
@ContextConfiguration(locations =
    {"classpath:dataModel.xml",
     "classpath:spring-test-datasource.xml"})
public class DomainModelTest {
  @Autowired PersonDao personDao;

  @Test
  public void testPerson() {
    // your business goes here
  }
}
```

Let's explore what's happening here. `@RunWith` tells JUnit that the test needs some extra logic in order to be set up with all of the things it needs. That extra logic comes in the form of an instance of a class that implements JUnit's `Runner` interface. In our case, we have a Spring `Runner` called `SpringJUnit4ClassRunner` that knows how to set up your application context and inject your test with all of the plumbing that it needs using the standard Spring dependency injection annotations, such as `@Autowired`. `SpringJUnit4ClassRunner` also looks for some other annotations to know how to set up the test including the `@ContextConfiguration` annotation and even the `@Transactional` annotation.

As you saw in the example, `@ContextConfiguration` tells `SpringJUnit4ClassRunner` which configuration files you need to set up your testing environment. Behind the scenes, `SpringJUnit4ClassRunner` sets up a `TestContext` that manages the Spring application context based on the locations you specified in the `@ContextConfiguration`. The `TestContext` is also responsible for actually performing the `@Autowired` injection. `TestContext` also keeps track of the results of the status of the current test, like which method and class were run and which exception, if any was thrown as part of the test.

Note   `TestContext` is used for both the JUnit infrastructure and the TestNG testing infrastructure. It has some performance optimizations to make sure that the `TestContext` will load that configuration only once for all of the tests if you run multiple test classes that use the same application context configuration.

`@RunWith` and `@ContextConfiguration` are the essential core components of Spring JUnit4 testing. There are quite a few additional advanced features relating to `TestContext` that will not be covered in this book but are worth exploring, if you have a need for more advanced testing. However, as a reader interested in persistence, it's important for you to know about some abstract base classes that give additional capabilities to your test. You can have access to the testing `ApplicationContext` by extending your test class from `AbstractJUnit4SpringContextTests` and use the protected `applicationContext` variable. There's a subclass of

AbstractJUnit4SpringContextTests,
AbstractTransactionalJUnit4SpringContextTests, that has some
database-specific testing utilities
(AbstractTransactionalJUnit4SpringContextTests also may have
an hold the record for the world's longest class name). The next section
describes it.

Testing with a Database

Now that you know how to write a JUnit test class and configure it with
Spring XML, you're ready to do some database testing! The simplest form
database testing can be to just reuse those fancy DAOs that you've been
working on. You can also apply the usual Spring @Transactional
annotations you've previously seen, along with another annotation,
@TransactionConfiguration. @TransactionConfiguration tells the
transactional Spring testing environment information about how to get the
transactionManager and whether you'd like to commit or roll back the
transaction after each test. Let's add those transactional annotations to the
test we created before:

```
@RunWith(SpringJUnit4ClassRunner.class)
@ContextConfiguration(locations =
    {"classpath:dataModel.xml",
     "classpath:spring-test-datasource.xml"})
@TransactionConfiguration(
   transactionManager = "transactionManager",
   defaultRollback = true)
@Transactional
public class DomainModelTest {
   @Autowired PersonDao personDao;

   @Test
   public void testPerson() {
      // your business goes here
      Person person = new Person();
```

```
    person.setFirstName("Paul");
    person.setLastName("Fisher");
    person.setUsername("pfisher");
    person.setPassword("password");
    person.setRoleLevel(Person.ADMIN);
    person.setVersion(1);
    personDao.savePerson(person);
    ...

  }
}
```

Congratulations! That's a working test. However, we have one more trick
to help with database testing. Remember the class with the long name we
talked about earlier? Recall that
`AbstractTransactionalJUnit4SpringContextTests` has access to the
`applicationContext`. Also, as long as you have a bean named
`dataSource`, you get an instance of `SimpleJdbcTemplate`. You can run
ad hoc queries against that instance to set up data in an `@Before` annotated
method or to verify that your DAO actually did what it was supposed to do.
`AbstractTransactionalJUnit4SpringContextTests` also defines
some testing specific SQL methods:

- `countRowsInTable`: As you'd expect, given the name of a table, this
  method gets a count of the number of rows. Here's an example:

  ```
  int peopleCount = countRowsInTable("person");
  ```

- `deleteFromTables`: This method deletes all rows from a list of tables. This
  method uses Java 5 varags, which allows you to send a variable number of
  arguments to a method, so you can call it with as many tables as you'd like.
  Here's an example:

  ```
  deleteFromTables("person", "comment");
  ```

- `executeSqlScript`: Use this method to run a script that is accessible
  through spring's `Resource` abstraction. This methods also takes a parameter
  specifying whether or not you'd like the testing to continue if there is an error
  in the script. Script files should consist of plain old SQL commands, one

command per line. For example, you can set up data in a @Before method like so:

```
executeSqlScript(
    "classpath:person_test_sql.txt",

    false);
```

Let's take our test for one more spin:

```
@RunWith(SpringJUnit4ClassRunner.class)
@ContextConfiguration(locations =
    {"classpath:dataModel.xml",
     "classpath:spring-test-datasource.xml"})
@TransactionConfiguration(
   transactionManager = "transactionManager",
   defaultRollback = true)
@Transactional
public class DomainModelTest extends
AbstractTransactionalJUnit4SpringContextTests {
   @Autowired PersonDao personDao;

   @Before
   public void testPerson() {
       // note, this is transactional, and will be
       // rolled back after the test completes
       deleteFromTables("person", "comment");
   }

   @Test
   public void testPerson() {
     Person person = new Person();
     person.setFirstName("Paul");
     person.setLastName("Fisher");
     person.setUsername("pfisher");
     person.setPassword("password");
     person.setRoleLevel(
        Person.RoleLevel.ADMIN.getLevel());
     person.setVersion(1);
```

```
        personDao.savePerson(person);

        // this is important. Without this, ORM DAOs
        // will not necessarily write out their changes
        // to the database
        personDao.flush();
        Assert.assertEquals(1, countRowsInTable("person"));
        // put more business logic here
    }
}
```

Summary

Of course, you can do a lot more to test with both JUnit and Spring. You can run mock tests or test with other database testing frameworks, such as DBUnit. And we've barely mentioned testing with TestNG. Also, topics such as performance testing and load testing are extremely relevant to persistence. Testing could probably be covered in a book all of its own, but alas, we have only one chapter. However, you've gotten a running start in testing databases with Spring.

Chapter 8: Using Spring with a Content Management System

A content management system (CMS) provides a higher level of abstraction than a standard relational database, offering features such as versioning, access control and authentication, searching, event notification, and workspace isolation. CMS integration is becoming more common as content management becomes a more integral aspect of web application development.

As CMS solutions grew in demand, the need for a standard in this area became more important. Several years ago, the specification for JSR-170 was approved, giving rise to a standard for CMS implementations: Java Content Repository (JCR).

Note   Java Specification Requests (JSRs) are proposed by members of the Java Community Process (JCP). All of the standards and reference implementations that have shaped the Java development world (such as JPA, JDBC, JEE, Java SE, and Servlet API) started as JSRs proposed by one or more members of the JCP. For more information, please visit the JCP web site at http://jcp.org/en/introduction/overview.

In this chapter, we'll look at integrating JCR with Spring, applying the design patterns and practices we've covered throughout this book. Although JCR provides a higher level of abstraction over persistence—along with numerous additional features that your application can easily leverage—the approach for integrating this technology is very similar to that of Hibernate or JDBC. We will cover the `JcrTemplate` and `JcrDaoSupport` classes that will help handle some of the boilerplate steps required for querying or persisting content to a CMS. We will use these framework classes for implementing our DAO layer. We will also create a service layer for delineating atomic business logic and apply transactional semantics using annotations and component scanning, again employing the strategies described in earlier chapters.

The biggest difference in our overall approach is the way in which our domain model is defined and implemented. Because JCR is focused on content, we are working at a different abstraction level than the other frameworks discussed in this book. As you'll learn shortly, JCR defines very specific rules for how content is stored within a CMS repository, based on a hierarchical tree of nodes and node properties.

Introducing JCR

JCR aims to provide a standard set of APIs that all CMS providers can implement, in order to be considered JCR compliant. Given the fair amount of differentiation among CMS implementations, the standard allows for several levels of compliancy. Level 1 contains core functionality, while Level 2 includes more specialized features. Additionally, providers may elect to implement a set of optional features that are also part of the standard. The JCR API includes methodology for determining the compliancy and supported feature set of an implementation, allowing developers to write code that can adapt to the any given CMS implementation at runtime. For instance, you could write code that determines whether the active JCR implementation was Level 1 or Level 2 compliant, allowing your application to dynamically activate or deactivate a set of features accordingly.

JCR is based on the concept of a node hierarchy. Content is organized into a node-based structure in which nodes may contain child nodes, similar to the way in which a directory can contain files within a filesystem.

Each node may contain a series of node properties. Properties are referenced by name and are used to represent strings, longs, doubles, dates, Booleans, paths, references (which point to other nodes in the workspace), and binary content (useful for image and audio data). Properties can be multivalued as well, so that an array of a particular data type may be stored within a single node property.

Developers may define custom node types to help delineate which properties and child nodes a given node can be expected to contain. Node types are somewhat analogous to Java classes in that they both serve to define a *type* representative of a particular data structure. However, JCR nodes are more flexible, as you can choose to create a node with a node type of nt:unstructured, allowing you to associate properties and child nodes in an arbitrary fashion. nt:unstructured is the default type used when an explicit node type is not specified. In architecting a JCR data model, developers can define custom node types or utilize some of the core node types that are part of the JCR specification. A given node type definition can specify supertypes from which to inherit along with the names and characteristics of each property or child node this type is allowed or required to contain. The JCR specification does not delineate a standard approach for defining custom node types, so each implementation might require a slightly different process. In the case of Apache Jackrabbit, the JCR reference implementation, node types are defined through CND files, which we will describe later in this chapter.

JCR nodes also support multiple inheritance, as a given node type can extend from multiple super types (although JCR implementations may differ in this regard). Furthermore, nodes may also be given new behavior and properties dynamically through the use of mix-in types, which decorate a node with additional features. In fact, mix-in types are the mechanisms used to imbue nodes with core CMS features, such as versioning, referencing, and locking, which we'll discuss shortly.

Architecting an application so that its content is organized into a clear, hierarchical structure can simplify the effort required to implement complex functionality. Due to its inherently hierarchical structure, JCR features several flexible approaches for querying content. Every node contains a UUID property, which serves as its unique identifier within the repository. Additionally, nodes may be looked up by specifying their path, which is their position within the repository hierarchy. However, the most effective querying approach is to use XPath notation, allowing nodes to be located based on their respective property values and path. The relative simplicity of JCR's organizational structure enables developers to implement functionality very quickly, since defining associations through foreign key relationships is not necessary. Instead, developers can model content into a hierarchy of nodes, child nodes, and properties.

A content store managed by JCR is called a *repository*. Each repository can contain one or more *workspaces* into which content can be sequestered. Not all applications will find workspaces useful, but workspaces are effective for providing preview, workflow, and isolation functionality, allowing content to be edited and verified within an isolated workspace and then merged to a production workspace once approved. For instance, we could give administrators of our gallery application their own workspaces, allowing them to edit, preview (as well as save and roll back to earlier versions), and merge images into a production workspace from which live content would be served to end users.

Introducing Spring Modules

Spring Modules is an open source project managed by the Spring team containing ancillary functionality that is not considered a core requirement of the Spring Framework itself. The project's aim is to provide Spring integration code for other popular frameworks and tools in the Java community. For instance, Spring Modules provides support for JCR, Lucene, JavaSpaces, OSWorkflow, Tapestry, and jBPM. The project also contains useful tools and extension points for Spring, including a powerful caching abstraction that simplifies application-level caching. Spring Modules is an often-overlooked gem, providing extremely useful functionality for several standards and popular frameworks. In this chapter, we will focus on Spring Modules's support for JCR, but we strongly recommend that you take a look at the Spring Modules project site at `https://springmodules.dev.java.net/` to see what else it can do.

Architecting Your Repository

Although it's conceivable to store any kind of data within a JCR repository, keep in mind that CMSs are intended primarily for content. So keeping with our gallery example, let's consider refactoring our architecture so that images (both image data and metadata) are now stored in a JCR repository rather than the database. This approach provides us with several key benefits. We will now be able to version changes to images, meaning we could provide administrators of our application with the ability to browse previous versions of a particular image and to roll back to an earlier version. Additionally, we can benefit from JCR's access control and event notification, allowing end users to be notified via e-mail when certain content is updated or added. We can also implement a search feature for our gallery application, allowing gallery users to easily search for an image by `title`, `displayDate`, `caption`, or any field property that we include in our design.

Although we gain these (and many other) features, our architecture becomes arguably cleaner and more intuitive. In our database-driven design, each image is represented by two tables: the `Art_Entity` table, which stores information about a particular image, and the `ArtData` table used to represent the image data itself. Our database design allows us to store several sizes of an image, using multiple rows in the `ArtData` table, each representing a particular image resolution. The `ArtData` table holds a foreign key reference back to the `Art_Entity` table, creating a bidirectional one-to-many/many-to-one relationship.

Following a JCR approach, we will design our content model using a node hierarchy. Every repository workspace has at least one node, called the *root node.* All content stems from this single root node, as every node within a JCR repository is required to have one (and only one) parent node. Since a JCR repository is inherently hierarchical, associations can be implicitly represented by adding child nodes to a particular node, in a similar fashion to the way a directory within a filesystem might contain multiple files or subdirectories.

For instance, to add multiple comments to an `ArtEntity` node, we simply need to call `artEntityNode.addNode("comment")` (for each comment added to the `artEntity`) in order to both define a new node (representing a comment's data) and create a parent-child relationship between the `artEntity` node and the child `comment` node.

Defining the JCR Data Model

For our gallery application, let's define a node with a name of `gallery:galleryImages` using the built-in node type of `nt:unstructured` that stems from the root node. This node would then be located at the following path: `/ROOT_NODE/gallery:galleryImages`.

Our `gallery:galleryImages` node will serve as the parent node under which all the `ArtEntity` nodes will be stored. We will represent each `ArtEntity` image using a node of node type `gallery:artEntity`. This node type will specify all the properties and their respective types required by nodes intended to represent a gallery image. In our case, we will define a node property for each respective field within our `ArtEntity` class (such as title, subtitle, width, height, and so on) and define child nodes to store the image data for the thumbnail, image, and archive sizes of each gallery image, respectively. Each respective image data child node will use the built-in node type `nt:resource` but will be located at different subpaths, stemming from a given `gallery:artEntity` node. For instance, the thumbnail image would be located at `/gallery:thumbnail`, while the archive image is located at path `/gallery:archive` (under a given node of type `gallery:artEntity`). Content management systems are intended to handle binary image and audio data, so storing images within the repository is a well-suited requirement for JCR.

Note   Don't confused node types and node names. Although both can utilize namespaces to avoid naming collisions, the former specifies a given node's characteristics, while the latter identifies part of a particular node's path within the repository.

We can also represent user comments as child nodes of a `gallery:artEntity` node. Each comment child node will be of node type `gallery:comment` and will contain node properties necessary to describe a particular comment, such as the comment text, comment date, and comment author. In this case, all comments can be given the same name of `comment`, since there is no important distinction between one comment and the next. Rather, our application will typically load all the comment child nodes together, in order to display the entire collection of comments below a particular image on the site. Each individual comment child node could be referenced by its index path, however. For instance, we could find the first comment of a given `ArtEntity` image by looking up a comment by its full path
`//jcr:root/gallery:galleryImages/<IMAGE_NODE_NAME>/comment`
`[1]` (where `<IMAGE_NODE_NAME>` represents the name of a `gallery:artEntity` node. You will learn how to actually load a given node using its path when we cover the `JcrTemplate`.

An important distinction between JCR and a database is that JCR associations are natural and implicit. Conversely, associations and collections within a relational database must be contrived through the use of foreign key relationships between multiple tables.

To make things clearer, Figure 8-1 illustrates how our repository will be modeled.

Figure 8-1. Content model for the gallery application using JCR

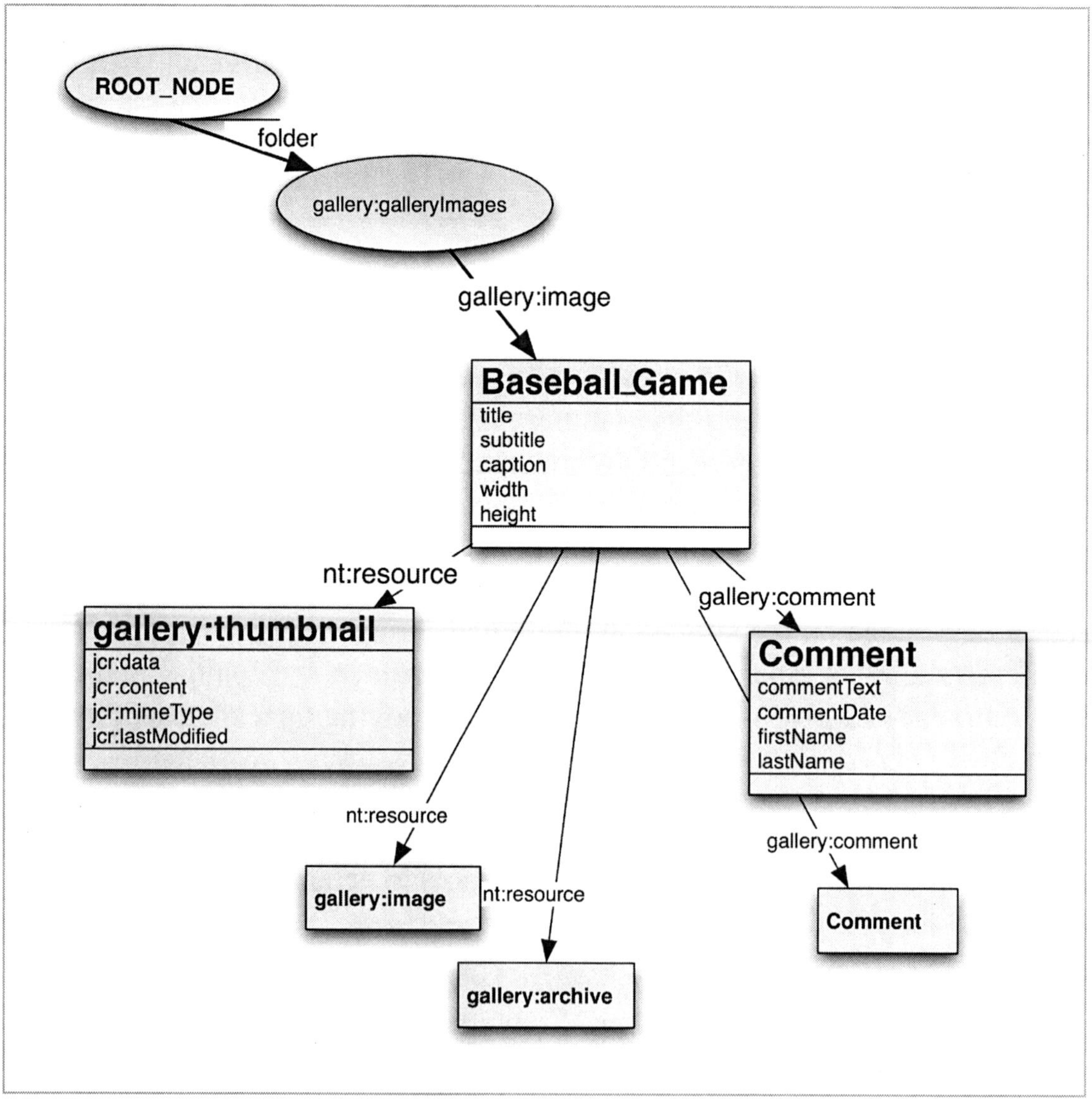

Starting from the top-left, Figure 8-1 shows the root node of our workspace. The next box represents the `gallery:galleryImages` node,

used primarily as a directory of sorts to contain and organize our `gallery:artEntity` nodes. Each `gallery:artEntity` node contains a set of `gallery:comment` child nodes, intended to represent comments, as well as `gallery:thumbnail`, `gallery:image`, and `gallery:archive` nodes, each of node type `nt:resource`, storing a particular resolution of image.

JCR has several predefined node types. It is common practice to designate a namespace using a prefix before a node type, name, or property, followed by a colon. Namespaces help to prevent name collisions within a repository. The `nt:` prefix is used to designate some of the common node types that have been defined within the JCR specification. `nt:resource` is used to represent a resource and is perfect for storing our image data. We will explain how to create an `nt:resource` node shortly.

Another predefined namespace is `mix`. As we discussed earlier, the `mix` namespace is special and designates behavior that can be dynamically *mixed in* to a particular node, hence it is known as the mix-in type. While node types help to classify a particular node, describing the properties and/or child nodes it contains, additional behavior (or properties) may be added to a particular node dynamically by injecting one or more mix-in types. In this way, you can enable behavior such as versioning (via the `mix:versionable` type) or locking support (via the `mix:lockable` type) for a particular node. Additionally, the `mix:reference` type allows a node to be referenceable. Once a node becomes referenceable, you can create associations to it from any other node by creating a node property of type reference and having its value point to the destination node. Again, this is another powerful capability of JCR, allowing associations to be created between nodes without having to consider a database table structure or foreign keys.

Getting Started with JCR

Now that you have a better grasp of how content is organized within a JCR repository, let's begin coding. This is where Spring Modules comes to our rescue. Spring Modules's JCR integration employs the patterns you have seen throughout this book. Based on Spring's ORM support, Spring Modules uses the template pattern as a means to minimize boilerplate code, as well as handle exceptions (converting them to Spring's consistent, unchecked `DataAccessException` hierarchy) and integrate Spring's standard transaction management. Not only does this simplify our code immensely but we also gain consistency and standardization, allowing us to integrate JCR in a manner that is very similar to other areas of our application.

To begin, we first need to initialize our JCR repository. Spring Modules provides several implementations of a `RepositoryFactoryBean`, designed to configure and instantiate a repository. Our example will use Apache Jackrabbit, the reference implementation for the JSR-170 specification. Jackrabbit is an Apache open-source project found at `http://jackrabbit.apache.org`. Before going further, download the latest version of Jackrabbit, and copy the included jars to your application's `lib` directory. You will also need the basic repository configuration file, which is set-up to work with a local Derby database by default (which simplifies installation). You should save the default `repository.xml` configuration and save it to the root of the application's `classpath`.

In our Spring configuration file, we can configure our `repositoryFactoryBean` as follows:

```
<bean id="jackrabbitRepository"
    class="org.springmodules.jcr. ⮠
jackrabbit.RepositoryFactoryBean">
  <property name="configuration" ⮠
    value="classpath:repository.xml"/>
  <property name="homeDir" ref="/repo"/>
</bean>
```

Following the factory bean pattern, the preceding configuration will create a Jackrabbit repository using the configuration specified in `repository.xml`, located at the root of our `classpath`. With our repository configured, we need to set up our `JcrSessionFactory`. If you look through the JCR specification, you won't find much information about `JcrSessionFactory`. That's because it's not actually part of the specification! Although the JCR API defines a `Session` interface for interfacing with the repository, there is no `SessionFactory` abstraction as there is in some of the ORM frameworks described in this book. `JcrSessionFactory` is a very useful construct defined by Spring Modules, allowing us to inject configuration data, such as credential details, which can in turn be used to retrieve new `Sessions` appropriately configured. Without Spring Modules, developers are forced to retrieve sessions directly, passing in credential information each time. Additionally, there are several operations that typically need to be applied to the entire repository, such as adding event listeners or defining namespaces. The `JcrSessionFactory` helps to streamline the retrieval of new sessions, as well as serve as an abstraction over the entire repository.

The JCR `Session` interface is very similar to the Hibernate `Session`: a new `Session` is created to perform a series of operations on the repository. When using Spring Modules, `Sessions` are created through the `JcrSessionFactory`, so let's first configure our `jcrSessionFactory` bean:

```xml
<bean id="jcrSessionFactory" ↪
  class="org.springmodules.jcr. ↪
jackrabbit.JackrabbitSessionFactory">
  <property name="repository" ↪
    ref=" jackrabbitRepository"/>
  <property name="credentials">
  <property name="nodeDefinitions">
     <list>
        <value>classpath:artEntity.cnd</value>
     </list>
  </property>
<property name="namespaces">
  <props>
   <prop key="gallery">
     http://dialmercury.com/gallery</prop>
     </props>
</property>
   <bean class="javax.jcr.SimpleCredentials">
    <constructor-arg index="0" value="pfisher"/>
    <!-- create the credentials
             using a bean factory -->
    <constructor-arg index="1">
     <bean factory-bean="passwordBean"
          factory-method="toCharArray"/>
    </constructor-arg>
   </bean>
  </property>
</bean>

<!-- create the password to
             return it as a char[] -->
<bean id="passwordBean" class="java.lang.String">
  <constructor-arg index="0" value="1234"/>
</bean>
```

The preceding configuration specifies the application's credential
information for accessing the repository and injects a reference to our
jackrabbitRepository bean defined earlier. The JCR specification

requires credential passwords to be passed in as a character array rather than a string (for security considerations). For this reason, we create a `passwordBean` with a class attribute of `java.lang.String` and invoke the `factory-method toCharArray` in order to convert this `String` reference to a character array so that it can be properly passed in to the `JcrSessionFactory`.

The property `namespaces` provides a centralized means for specifying the custom namespaces we will be using in our repository. In our example, we have defined a single namespace prefix of `gallery`. Notice that we also inject a list into the `nodeDefinitions` property. This property is actually a feature of the `JackrabbitSessionFactory` class (we could choose to use the more generic `JcrSessionFactory` class instead, if we didn't need this Jackrabbit-specific feature). The `nodeDefinitions` property takes a list of file paths, pointing to custom node type definitions in the CND format. For our gallery application, we have defined two custom node types: `gallery:artentity` and `gallery:comment`. CND is a concise way of specifying those properties and child nodes a particular node type can be expected to contain. The CND representation of our `gallery:artentity` node type can be described as follows:

```
<gallery = 'http://dialmercury.com/gallery'>
[gallery:artentity] > nt:unstructured
  orderable
  - gallery:title (string)
    primary mandatory
    version
  - gallery:subtitle (string) version
  - gallery:uploadedDate (date) mandatory
  - gallery:displayDate (string)
  - gallery:width (long)
  - gallery:height (long)
  - gallery:media (string)
  - gallery:description (string)
  - gallery:caption (string)
```

```
- gallery:generalViewable (boolean)
- gallery:privilegeViewable (boolean)
- gallery:categories (string) multiple
+ gallery:thumbnail (nt:resource)
+ gallery:image (nt:resource)
+ gallery:archive (nt:resource)
+ comment(gallery:comment) multiple
```

An in-depth discussion of the CND format is outside the scope of this book, however, we will point out some important details. The second line in the preceding example defines the name of our node type, indicating that it extends the built-in type `nt:unstructured`. Lines that begin with a minus sign define a node property, while lines starting with a plus sign represent a child node. For example, the preceding example indicates that our `gallery:artentity` node type will have a node property with the name `gallery:title` and that this property is of type `String` and is required. We also indicate that we can have multiple sibling child nodes with the name `comment`, and that these child nodes should be of type `gallery:comment`.

With our `JcrSessionFactory` defined, we are ready to begin working with our repository. Similar to Hibernate, JCR provides a `Session` interface through which we can manipulate and access the repository. And similar to Spring's `HibernateTemplate`, Spring Modules offers a `JcrTemplate` for handing boilerplate JCR operations, such as retrieving a new `Session` from the `JcrSessionFactory`, converting exceptions to Spring's unchecked `DataAccessException` hierarchy, and integrating transaction management.

Now, let's define our `JcrTemplate`:

```
<bean id="jcrTemplate"
  class="org.springmodules.jcr.JcrTemplate">
  <property name="sessionFactory" ref="sessionFactory"/>
  <property name="allowCreate" value="false"/>
</bean>
```

The preceding bean will instantiate a new JcrTemplate, injecting the
JcrSessionFactory we defined previously. With configuration out of the
way, let's create our first JCR DAO. We will call our class
JcrArtEntityDao:

```
public class JcrArtEntityDao extends JcrDaoSupport{

public Node saveArtEntity(final ArtEntity artEntity){
    Node artNode = (Node) this.getTemplate()
          .execute(new JcrCallback() {
    public Object doInJcr(Session session)
        throws RepositoryException {
        // create instance of jcrConstants
        JcrConstants jcrConstants =
         new JcrConstants(session);
      // get access to the root node
      Node root = session.getRootNode();
        Node galleryNode = null;
      //check to see if our gallery:galleryImages
      // node is already created; if not, create it
      if (root.hasNode("gallery:galleryImages")) {
        galleryNode.getNode("gallery:galleryImages");
      } else {
          galleryNode =
              root.addNode("gallery:galleryImages");
      }
      // we use the artEntity title field for our
      // node name. Make sure it's JCR safe.
      String artEntityNodeName =
          ArtEntity.jcrSafeName(artEntity.getTitle());
      Node artEntityNode = null;
      // check to see if we've already created a
```

```java
// node for this artEntity. If so, load it,
// otherwise create it.
if (galleryNode.hasNode(artEntityNodeName)) {
  artEntityNode =
     galleryNode.getNode(artEntityNodeName);
} else {
    // create a new node, using our safe-title
    // as the name, and a node type of
    // gallery:artentity
    artEntityNode =
       galleryNode.addNode(
          artEntityNodeName,
          "gallery:artentity"
       );
    // we want our artentity nodes to be
    // versionable, so we need to add the
    // mixin:version
    artEntityNode.
     addMixin(jcrConstants.getMIX_VERSIONABLE());
}
// since this is a versionable node, we need
// to checkout before changing properties
artEntityNode.checkout();
artEntityNode.setProperty(
   "title", artEntity.getTitle());
artEntityNode.setProperty(
   "subTitle", artEntity.getSubTitle());
artEntityNode.setProperty(
   "caption", artEntity.getCaption());
artEntityNode.setProperty(
   "description", artEntity.getDescription());
artEntityNode.setProperty(
   "displayDate", artEntity.getDisplayDate());
artEntityNode.setProperty(
   "width", artEntity.getWidth());
artEntityNode.setProperty(
   "height", artEntity.getHeight());
// iterate through each comment in our
```

```java
// artEntity domain class
for (Comment comment : artEntity.getComments()){
  // create a new comment node with name comment
  // Since we're defining multiple child nodes
  // with the same name, they will need to be
  // referenced by index, such as: comment[1]

  // NOTE: We should also have logic to load and
  // edit existing comments, but for the sake of
  // brevity, we have simplied this example.
  // Please check-out the full source-code
  // on-line at the book's website.
  Node commentNode =
    artEntityNode.addNode(
          "comment", "gallery:coment"
    );
  commentNode.setProperty(
    "comment", comment.getComment());
  Calendar commentCal = Calendar.getInstance();
  commentCal.setTime(comment.getCommentDate());
  commentNode.setProperty(
    "commentDate", commentCal);
  commentNode.setProperty(
    "firstName", comment.getFirstName());
  commentNode.setProperty(
    "lastName", comment.getLastName());
}
// Create or load our thumbnail child node
// which is of type nt:resource
Node resourceNode = null;
if (artEntityNode.hasNode("gallery:thumbnail")) {
    resourceNode =
      artEntityNode.getNode("gallery:thumbnail");
} else {
  resourceNode =
      artEntityNode.addNode(
        "gallery:thumbnail",
        jcrConstants.getNT_RESOURCE()
```

```
        );
      }
      resourceNode.setProperty(
        jcrConstants.getJCR_DATA(),
        new ByteArrayInputStream(
          artEntity.getGalleryThumbnail() ↪
            .getPicture())));
      resourceNode.setProperty(
        jcrConstants.getJCR_MIMETYPE(),
        "application/octet-stream");
      resourceNode.setProperty(
        jcrConstants.getJCR_ENCODING(), "");
      resourceNode.setProperty(
        jcrConstants.getJCR_LASTMODIFIED(),
      Calendar.getInstance());
      artEntityNode.checkin();
      session.save();
      return artEntityNode;
    }
  });
  return artNode;
}
```

In the preceding example, we use JcrTemplate's execute() method, passing in an anonymous inner class that implements the JcrCallback interface. The JcrTemplate will handle the JCR Session retrieval and exception handling, allowing us to just focus on creating our nodes.

You can see from the example just how intuitive it is to add our image content. We start by finding the root node, using the getRootNode() method. We next use the Node interface to find our galleryImages, via getNode(String), passing in the name of our directory node. If this node hasn't yet been created, we create it by calling addNode() on the root node. After that, we create our gallery:artentity node by calling addNode() on the galleryImages node, passing in the title of our image, which will be used to specify the name of our new gallery:artentity node. This method returns a new `Node` reference, onto which we can set all the necessary properties defined by our custom `gallery:artentity` node type. The rest of the method should be fairly straightforward. We iterate through each field within our `ArtEntity` domain class, setting the related property on our node reference. We define new comments by creating child nodes of type `gallery:comment` and name `comment` and setting the associated properties for each individual `comment` node.

It is also important to point out how we store our image data. We create a new child node of type `nt:resource`, which is used to store the image data along with basic metadata about the binary data. Spring Modules provides a `JcrConstants` class, which abstracts JCR-related names to ensure that changes to the specification won't require numerous code changes. In our example, we only add one `nt:resource` child node to represent a thumbnail image, but we would normally create multiple `nt:resource` nodes to represent each image resolution type.

Finally, since we want our gallery images to be versioned, we save our node by invoking `artEntityNode.checkin()`, followed by `session.save()`. To ensure a node is versionable, we must call `artEntityNode.addMixin("mix:versionable")` when it is first created, decorating the node with versionable behavior. Additionally, we must also call `artEntity.checkout()` and `artEntity.checkin()` before and after altering properties of the versionable node.

From an architecture perspective, the entire flow is very reminiscent of Spring's Hibernate support, allowing us to repurpose much of our knowledge in this area.

Querying for JCR Nodes

We've demonstrated how intuitive creating new nodes and child nodes can be using JCR. However, we've only demonstrated basic querying functionality through the use of the `Node.getNode()` method. This feature allows us to access a node by specifying its relative path from the vantage point of the node on which `getNode()` is invoked. For instance, you could access a particular comment of a `gallery:artentity` node named "baseball" as follows:

```
Node rootNode = Session.getRootNode();
Node coolComment =
  rootNode.getNode(
  "gallery:galleryImages/baseball/comment[1]"
);
```

Accessing a node directly through its path is very powerful, however, it is often important to be able to query for a collection of nodes based on a series of criteria. Using XPath, we can express a conditional query based on one or more of a node's properties. For example, suppose we wanted to load all nodes that contain the word baseball in the `gallery:description` property. This query could be expressed as follows:

```
//*[jcr:like(@gallery:description, '%baseball%')]
```

The preceding query will find the token baseball anywhere within the `gallery:description` property. We could also express this query as follows, which will look for the specific word baseball:

```
//*[jcr:contains(@gallery:description, 'baseball')]
```

Or, if we wanted to require that we only loaded those nodes within the `gallery:galleryImages` path, we could add a specific node path constraint:

```
//gallery:galleryImages/*[jcr:contains( ➥
@gallery:description, 'baseball')]
```

Now that you have a better understanding of how to define a JCR query using XPath, let's implement another DAO method that will allow us to find all `gallery:artentity` nodes that have a specified `subtitle`. Our method can be defined as follows:

```java
public List findArtBuSubtitle(String subtitle) {
   // define an XPath query,
   // using the gallery:subtitle
   // as a constraint
   QueryResult result = this.getTemplate().
     query("//*[@gallery:subtitle = " + subtitle + "]");
     List foundArtEntities = new ArrayList();
     try {
       // get a NodeIterator from
      // the returned QueryResult
       NodeIterator nodeIt = result.getNodes();
       while (nodeIt.hasNext()) {
          Node curNode = (Node) nodeIt.next();
          // Here we convert the returned node back
          // to an ArtEntity instance (method not shown)
          ArtEntity artEntity = nodeToArtEntity(curNode);
          // add the converted ArtEntity to our List
          foundArtEntities.add(artEntity);
       }
    } catch (RepositoryException e) {
       // Here we convert any Jcr
       // RepositoryException into Spring's
       // unchecked DataAccessException hierarchy
       throw this.convertJcrAccessException(e);
    }
    return foundArtEntities;
}
```

In the preceding example, we use the `JcrTemplate`'s query method to
execute an XPath query, returning an instance of the `QueryResult` class.
We then use the `QueryResult` instance to get a `NodeIterator`, with
which we iterate in order to load each successive node returned by the
query. We convert each node back to an `ArtEntity` instance to shield the
application from our JCR-based implementation (the conversion method
isn't shown, but quite simply, it gets each node property and sets the
appropriate field in our `ArtEntity` class). It's important to point out that
although certain operations may throw checked JCR

`RepositoryExceptions`, it is good practice to convert them to Spring's consistent, unchecked `DataAccessException` hierarchy. In the preceding example, we accomplish this using the `JcrDaoSupport` class's `convertJcrAccessException()` method.

Defining Our Service Layer

Now that we've created our DAO, we should consider transactional support. Spring Modules allows us to integrate a standard `TransactionManager`—just like we've used with other persistence technologies. We recommend following the service facade pattern we've discussed throughout this book. Our service class will then contain a Spring-injected reference to our `ArtEntityDao`. Next, we can add `@Transaction` annotations in exactly the same manner followed in earlier chapters. However, to glue everything together, we will need to add the following Spring configuration, in order to bootstrap our annotation-based transaction support:

```
<bean id="jcrTransactionManager"
class="org.springmodules.jcr.jackrabbit. ↪
LocalTransactionManager">
    <property name="sessionFactory"
      ref="jcrSessionFactory"/>
</bean>
<context:component-scan
  base-package="com.smartpants.artwork.dao.jcr"> ↪
  <context:include-filter type="annotation"
  expression="org.springframework.stereotype. ↪
Repository"/>
</context:component-scan>
<context:component-scan
      base-package="com.smartpants.artwork.service">
  <context:include-filter type="annotation"
      expression="org.springframework. ↪
stereotype.Service"/>
```

```
</context:component-scan>
<tx:annotation-driven ↪
    transaction-manager="jcrTransactionManager"/>
```

The preceding configuration instantiates a `LocalTransactionManager` for Jackrabbit and injects it into the annotation-driven `TranasactionManager`. We've also added two component scanners: one for our JCR DAO package and another for our service facade class, which will contain the `@Transaction` annotations and delegate to our `JcrArtEntityDao`. It is important that we define our service class to be in the `com.smartpants.artwork.service` package. Although we won't provide examples of the service class here, it should work in roughly the same fashion as in earlier chapters: we define a service implementation and interface and place `@Transaction` annotations above each service-layer method. Spring will take care of the rest! For more information about implementing a transactional service layer, please refer to Chapters 3 and 6.

Summary

Throughout this book, you've seen the same core persistence design patterns played out repeatedly. Specifically, you've learned how Spring helps to provide consistency and modularization to an application through the DAO, template, and facade patterns. In this chapter, you've learned how JCR, a standard for working with content management systems, can serve to simplify even complex data models. JCR provides a higher level of abstraction over the persistence technologies we've discussed throughout this book, providing features such as versioning, authentication, search, event listeners, workspace isolation, and much more.

Next, we'll look at Grails, and GORM, which rely on the Spring Framework but utilize a different set of patterns for persistence than the strategies we've discussed over the course of this book.

Chapter 9: Rapid Web Development Using Groovy and Grails

GORM is Grail's answer to ORM. Essentially, it is an ORM framework based on Groovy. At the foundation of GORM lies the same strategy responsible for Ruby on Rails's success: convention over configuration. GORM drastically simplifies the amount of coding and effort required to define your application's persistence logic. With GORM and Grails, there is no need to define a DAO layer. Instead, the active record design pattern (which we'll discuss shortly) is employed, consolidating persistence functionality into the domain class itself. This may seem a bit like magic, but you'll learn how GORM works under the hood by tapping into the dynamic features of Groovy.

Note   *GORM* is the name of the persistence component within Grails. Although GORM can also be used outside a Grails application, for the sake of simplicity, we will use the terms *GORM* and *Grails* interchangeably throughout this chapter.

Grails and GORM came onto the scene as a result of the attention brought about by the success of the Ruby on Rails framework. Ruby on Rails took the mantras of "convention over configuration" and "don't repeat yourself (DRY)" to a new level, significantly simplifying the effort required to create a new web application.

Some of Ruby on Rails's success stems from the fact that Ruby is a dynamic language, which brings a level of flexibility that is not easily attainable in the Java world. For instance, the capability to dynamically invoke behavior at runtime, based on the naming convention of an attempted method call can't be easily replicated in Java code because it doesn't natively support the dynamic creation of new methods. Luckily, Groovy came onto the scene to bring this flexibility to the Java world.

Note   *DRY* stands for "don't repeat yourself" (oops, it looks like we just did).

Groovy is a dynamic language that runs in the JVM. This means that Groovy code can be easily compiled to Java bytecode. More importantly, it also means that Groovy can utilize Java libraries, making the myriad open source Java libraries accessible to this new language.

Some may argue that Grails does not quite fit into a book about Spring persistence. However, the Grails framework and GORM rely heavily on the Spring framework, as well as Hibernate, for much of the flexibility and persistence magic they afford. The benefits of this heritage are the longevity, enterprise strength, efficiency, and flexibility offered by Spring and Hibernate (as well as the core Java/JEE stack). Furthermore, G2One, the company behind much of the Grails and Groovy development, was recently acquired by SpringSource, giving a clear indication that SpringSource is vested in the future of Grails and Groovy.

Now that you've got the background in place, let's start setting up our Grails environment.

Getting Grails Running

The Grails persistence solution is so dramatically different from the other DAO-based persistence solutions that you've seen earlier (you'll learn what these differences are later in this chapter) that we can't really build on our existing demonstration code, as we've done throughout this book. Instead, we need to start over and architect our gallery application using the Grails approach. This may seem like a daunting task at first, but Grails comes with many shortcut templates and scripts designed to actually start stubbing out code for you!

But first, we need to install Grails. Head over to `http://www.grails.org`, and download the latest release. Unzip the downloaded archive, and copy everything to a logical location on your hard drive. Next, make sure that everything under the `bin` directory is executable. If you're using a Unix-based OS, you can run `chmod ug+x ./*` from within the `bin` directory. Also, you need to make sure the `GRAILS_HOME` and `JAVA_HOME` environment variables are set up. `GRAILS_HOME` should point to the location where you installed Grails. Also, make sure that you've added the `GRAILS_HOME/bin` directory to your `PATH`, so that you don't need to specify the full path to the Grails executables each time you want to invoke a Grails script.

If you are using a Unix-based operating system, I recommend updating your `.bashrc` script within your home directory so that you don't need to do this configuration more than once. On a Mac, you can append the following lines to `.bashrc`:

```
export JAVA_HOME= ➥
/System/Library/Frameworks/JavaVM.framework/Home/
export GRAILS_HOME=/Users/paul/Tools/grails-1.0.4/
export PATH=$PATH:$GRAILS_HOME/bin
```

Once you've got everything ready to go, the next step is to create our gallery application. As mentioned earlier, Grails ships with scripts that take care of generating boilerplate code to get your application started. The first of these scripts that we will introduce is the `create-app` script:

```
grails create-app gallery
```

In the preceding example, we pass `gallery` as the only argument. Grails will churn for a few seconds, and voilà! You now have a new Grails application set up and ready to go. Part of the convention-over-configuration concept is organizing and naming key parts of your application in a standardized way. The `create-app` script makes this easy by setting up the Grails directory structure for you.

Exploring the Grails Application Directory Structure

After the `create-app` script completes, you will end up with the following directory structure:

```
gallery ->
    grails-app
        conf
            spring
                resources.groovy
            Bootstrap.groovy
            Datasource.groovy
            Urlmappings.groovy
        controllers
        domain
        i18n
        services
        taglib
        utils
        views

    scripts
    src
        java
        groovy
    test
        integration
        unit
    web-app
        css
        js
        images
        WEB-INF
        index.gsp
```

Most of our coding effort will be focused on the `grails-app` directory, which is where the majority of our Groovy code will live. Before we start getting our hands dirty, let's take a brief tour of the Grails application layout.

Let's begin with the `grails-app` directory. Not surprisingly, the `grails-app/conf` directory holds the application's configuration. Grails was designed to be very modular in nature, so it isn't always necessary to explicitly configure each one of your dependencies. However, since Grails is really a Spring application at its core, the `grails-app/conf/spring/resources.groovy` file can be used to configure your dependencies. Although this is a spring configuration file, you'll notice that it isn't an XML format. Grails provides a custom domain-specific language (DSL) to configure your Spring beans, and since this file is essentially executable Groovy code, it can be a lot more flexible than a standard XML-based configuration.

Note   The default configuration approach uses a `resources.groovy` file, though you could instead create a `resources.xml` file, which allows the use of the more-standard XML-based configuration.

Using the Spring DSL is fairly straightforward. As an example, let's suppose we wanted to create an e-mail service, so that we can notify end-users via e-mail when new images are added to the gallery. We might want to configure the Spring e-mail–sending component within our `resources.groovy` file so that it can be utilized within our application. Here is how this configuration might look:

```
beans = {
    javaMailSender(
org.springframework.mail.javamail.JavaMailSenderImpl) {
        host = 'smtp.dialmercury.com'
    }
}
```

The pattern is fairly intuitive: the bean name is defined first, followed by
the class name within parentheses. Properties within the bean are then
configured within a closure block, which is the part of the code within
curly braces ({}). Closures are a key foundational concept within groovy,
and we will be discussing them shortly.

If we wanted to inject our `javaMailSender` bean into a Grails service or
controller, we can simply rely on default autowiring by name, by declaring
a property named `javaMailSender` within the appropriate Grails service
or controller class:

```
class EmailService {
    def javaMailSender
}
```

Similarly, if we wanted to reference our Grails `EmailService` within
another bean configured within our `resources.groovy` file, we would
need to reference it using its implicit bean name. In this case, it would be
`emailService`. For instance, we might define a `NotificationComponent`
bean within our `resources.groovy` file as follows:

```
beans = {
    notificationComponent(
com.dialmercury.NotificationComponent) {bean ->
        emailService = ref("emailService")
        bean.factoryMethod = "getInstance"
        bean.singleton = "false"
        defaultNotificationMethods = ["email", "sms"]
    }
}
```

Notice that we've declared a bean parameter at the top of the block using `bean ->`. This convention will become clearer once we discuss closures later in this chapter. The important thing to remember, however, is that by declaring a bean parameter, we are able to specify more explicit details related to the type of bean we are trying to configure. In this case, we specified a `factoryMethod` of `getInstance`, which ensures that new instances of this bean will be instantiated by calling `getInstance()`. We have also specified that this is not a `singleton` bean.

Also notice that we have injected a reference to our `EmailService` by using the convention `ref("BEANNAME")`, in which `BEANNAME` is the name of our `EmailService` bean. We are able to apply most of our Spring configuration knowledge to this more flexible Groovy-based DSL. However, notice the flexibility advantage over XML in the following example:

```
beans = {
   javaMailSender(
org.springframework.mail.javamail.JavaMailSenderImpl) {
      if (grails.util.GrailsUtil.environment == ↪
             "production") {
       host = 'smtp.dialmercury.com'
      } else {
        host = "smtp.dev.dialmercury.com"
      }
    }
  }
```

Clearly, interpretable code has its benefits over static XML. In fact, this overview only touches on some of the configuration options for Grails. It is also possible to configure dynamic bean names, as well as specify property placeholder and override configuration. For more information, please take a look at the Grails documentation.

Booting Up

The `grails-app/conf/Bootstrap.groovy` file provides simple hooks (`init()` and `destroy()`) for handling application start-up and shutdown events. During development, `Bootstrap.groovy` is an effective means for seeding your application's database with default data.

Configuring Your Application

The `grails-app/Config.groovy` file is a centralized location for specifying key configuration details about your Grails application. This file contains information about the character encoding your application should use, as well as logging details (using log4j).

Grails leverages the innate concept of environments to facilitate the creation and separation of different development and deployment scenarios. For instance, you will likely need to use a different database (requiring variant configuration details) for development or testing than you would for your production deployment. These concepts are built into the Grails core, making it easy to test with a development database and deploy your application to production for use with the live database—without having to remember to swap out the configuration. Environment-specific details are present in several key configuration files.

The `Config.groovy` file contains an initial block of code to specify the default `serverURL` for production:

```
environments {
    production {
        grails.serverURL = "http://www.changeme.com"
    }
}
```

If you wanted to specify a different URL for development, you might modify the configuration snippet accordingly:

```
environments {
  production {
    grails.serverURL = "http://www.mycoolgallery.com"
  }
  development {
    grails.serverURL = "http://dev.mycoolgallery.com"
  }
}
```

Also, keep in mind that there is no constraint on the types of environments your application defines or uses. You can add as many additional types of environments as you see fit.

Configuring Your Datasource

Since most web applications require a database, Grails defines a file specifically for configuring datasource-related details: `Datasource.groovy`. This file also uses a custom Groovy-based DSL, making this configuration clear and concise. The environment concept is built into this file as well. Properties can be configured at a global level if they apply to all environments. Environment-specific configuration, however, should be nested within the appropriate environment block. In the case of our gallery application, here's what our `Datasource.groovy` file might look like (keep in mind that most of this file is already created for you; you only need to configure the details that are specific to your application):

```
dataSource {
    pooled = true
    driverClassName = "org.hsqldb.jdbcDriver"
    username = "sa"
    password = ""
}
hibernate {
    cache.use_second_level_cache=true
    cache.use_query_cache=true
        cache.provider_class= ↪
```

```
    'com.opensymphony.oscache.hibernate.OSCacheProvider'
    }
// environment specific settings
environments {
    development {
        dataSource {
            dbCreate = "create-drop"
            url = "jdbc:hsqldb:mem:gallerydb_dev"
        }
    }
    test {
        dataSource {
            dbCreate = "update"
            url = "jdbc:hsqldb:mem:gallerydb_test"
        }
    }
    production {
        dataSource {
            dbCreate = "update"
            url = ➥
    "jdbc:hsqldb:file:gallerydb_prod;shutdown=true"
        }
    }
```

Notice that the dataSource property is specified at the top of the file as
well as within the environments block. Global details, such as database
connection pooling settings and the JDBC driver, are configured globally
by placing these details within a top-level dataSource block.
Environment-specific details, such as the database URL for the
development, test, and production environments respectively, are
configured within the dataSource blocks within their respective
environments. However, if we needed to use a different JDBC driver for
production, we could either move these details within the appropriate
environment blocks or simply override the globally configured details
within the appropriate environment. Again, the types of environments you

can configure are not restricted: `development`, `test`, and `production` are just default environments created by the Grails templates.

Mapping URLs

The last file we need to cover in the `grails-app/conf` directory is `UrlMappings.groovy`. This file provides an amazingly flexible construct for associating URL patterns with a particular controller and action. We'll cover the details of how this works later in this chapter, but as a preliminary example, here's how we might relate the pretty URL `/category/panoramas` with the `CategoryController`, specifying that the `panaromas` category be displayed:

```
class UrlMappings {
    static mappings = {
        "/$controller/$action?/$id?"{
            constraints {

            }
        }
        "/category/$categoryName"
  (controller: CategoryController,
    action: "displayCategory")
        "500"(view:'/error')
    }
}
```

The mapping we described is actually the second block in the preceding example. The first component of the mapping is the part in quotes. We are essentially defining a regular expression that starts with `/category/`. The `$categoryName` defines a parameter name that will automatically be passed to your controller, using the specified chunk of the URL at which the parameter name resides. In the preceding example, the part of the URL after `/category/` will be extracted and then stored in the parameter named `categoryName`.

If you look at the first block in the preceding example, you will notice the default URLMapping. In this scenario, we are defining $controller and $action parameters; these are special keywords, and instead of denoting a particular parameter, they define the controller to which the matching request should be directed, as well as the corresponding action. In our category listing page example, we haven't defined a $controller within our mapping expression, so we instead specify this explicitly, the following way:

```
(controller: CategoryController,
    action: " displayCategory")
```

We haven't really defined what controllers and actions actually are, but we'll get to these details in our discussion of the Grails application layers, which we'll cover next.

Exploring the Grails Application Layers

Grails is composed of three core layers, which resemble the tiers we've discussed earlier in this book:

- Domain
- Controller
- Service

To provide consistency and better enforce convention, Grails enforces a directory structure to help organize and sequester classes from each respective layer. The domain model typically serves as the foundation for a Grails application and therefore is typically the first layer to be defined.

As you probably already guessed, the domain model classes all go into the grails-app/domain directory. By default, all domain classes will live in the default Grails package. However, you are free to define your own package structure, and for larger applications, this is especially recommended. Additionally, if you will need to access any of your Grails code from Java, you will need to keep your Grails classes within a package, or it will be difficult to access them outside the Grails/Groovy world.

Tip   You can also have your Groovy classes implement an interface that is accessible to Java, as a means to better integrate your Grails code with Java.

Defining Your Domain Model

Let's begin our Grails-based gallery application by defining our `Person` domain entity. Grails provides scripts to help create most of the core Grails archetypes, each corresponding to a particular template. You are also free to edit these templates if you want to change the way your default views or domain and service classes are created. To do this, you will need to run `grails install-templates`. You will then be able to access (and modify) the templates from within the `src/templates` directory. However, for most Grails development, the default templates are just fine.

To create our `Person` domain class, we will need to run

```
grails create-domain-class
```

Once this script completes, you will find a `Person.groovy` class within the `grails-app/domain` directory. Grails uses Hibernate behind the scenes to persist `Person` instances to, and retrieve them from, the database. Unlike Hibernate, no mapping files or annotations are required, since convention helps Grails infer most of what it needs to handle persistence for your domain model.

Now that we've created our stub for our `Person` domain entity, let's define the rest of the properties:

```
class Person {
    String firstName;
    String lastName;
    String username;
    String password;
    String emailAddress;
    Integer roleLevel;

    static constrants = {
        firstName(maxSize:255, unique: false,
                blank: false)
        lastName(maxSize:255, unique: false,
                blank: false)
        username(maxSize:255, unique: true,
                blank: false)
        password(maxSize:25, unique: false,
                blank: false)
        emailAddress(emailAddress: true,
                blank: false, unique: false)
    }

    static mapping = {
        cache true

    }

}
```

The first thing you will probably notice in the preceding example is just how concise this code is. Most of the properties should be self-explanatory. Since we are using Groovy, there is no need to define getters or setters (these are implicit within Groovy). You will also notice that there are no properties specified for id or version; these fields are automatically created for you by Grails.

Defining Constraints and Validation

Let's now look at the `constraints` block. Constraints allow you to better define each field within your domain model, providing clues and requirements to Grails as to how your database schema should be modeled. A number of constraint options are available, but here some of the most useful:

- `blank`
- `minSize`
- `maxSize`
- `range`
- `unique`
- `size`
- `range`
- `inList`
- `email`
- `creditCard`
- `matches`
- `nullable`

Some of these constraints can be extremely powerful. For example, the `matches` constraint allows you to specify a regular expression that will be used to validate the value in the specified field, ensuring it matches the specified regular expression.

The domain-specific constraints, such as `email` and `creditCard`, will help to ensure that your field conforms to a valid e-mail address or credit card number, respectively.

There are actually quite a few more constraints than those listed, and Groovy includes a construct that allows you to define your own. The syntax for defining a constraint for a particular property is pretty straightforward. You specify the property, followed by a mapping of constraint types and their corresponding values, for example:

```
username(blank: false, maxSize: 255, unique: true)
```

This will ensure that the `username` value cannot be left blank and that the database field has a maximum size of 255 characters. Additionally, a `unique` constraint will also be added to the `username` database field.

Constraints come into play when you attempt to save a domain entity to the database. If a particular field is not validated, an error will be attached to a dynamic `errors` property on your domain instance. Additionally, the constraints defined for each property, coupled with a consistent naming convention, are assembled into error message codes that are automatically used within the default Grails GSP (Groovy Server Pages) templates. For example, if you attempt to save a `Person` entity without specifying a `username`, a validation error will be raised and associated within the instance's `errors` property. Afterward, this error will be properly rendered within the default GSP template (which we'll discuss shortly), using an error code that is defined in the application's `messages.properties` resource bundle. When a validation error code is found, Grails will attempt to look for the appropriate code within the `messages.properties` file, starting with the most specific naming convention and moving toward the more generic conventions, until a match is found. This ensures that if you don't bother adding a specific error code in your `messages.properties` file, users will still see a sensible error (something to the effect that the `blank` constraint for the `username` field has been violated). However, you can easily override this default message by specifying a `blank` constraint error code that's specific to the `Person` class.

Defining Associations and Properties on Your Domain Model

The `Person` domain entity is a fairly simplistic example, as it doesn't really contain any associations or customized mappings. Let's take a look at a more complex entity to see how Grails addresses a more typical scenario. First, we'll examine the `Comment` class:

```
class Comment {
     String comment;
     Date commentDate;
     Person person;

     static belongsTo = [commentedArt: ArtEntity]

     static constraints = {
            comment(maxSize: 2000, blank: false)
            commentDate(nullable: false)
        }

     static mapping = {
        cache true
        }
  }
```

This class is similar to the `Person` entity we defined earlier. We've defined a few properties, as well as a `constraints` block. One addition, however, is the `belongsTo` field. The `belongsTo` field provides clues to Grails about the relationship between two entities. In this example, we are defining a parent-child relationship between a `Comment` and an `ArtEntity`. We are also defining a property called `commentedArt` and declaring that this property is of type `ArtEntity`. We could also choose to specify additional `belongsTo` relationships by appending them to this map. In each case, however, the `key` represents the property name, while the `value` represents the type.

The use of belongsTo also asserts cascading rules. In the previous example, we are declaring that ArtEntity is the parent in this relationship, meaning save and delete operations (on ArtEnity) will cascade appropriately to related Comment instances. This relationship will become clearer after we examine the opposing side, the ArtEntity domain class:

```
class ArtEntity {

    String title;
    String subTitle;
    Date uploadedDate;
    Date displayDate;
    int width;
    int height;
    String media;
    String description;
    String caption;
    ArtData_Gallery galleryPicture;
    ArtData_Storage storagePicture;
    ArtData_Thumbnail thumbnailPicture;
    boolean isGeneralViewable;
    boolean isPrivilegeViewable;

    static hasMany =
      [categories: Categories, comments: Comment]
  static belongsTo = Category

    static constraints = {
        title(blank:false, maxSize: 255)
        subTitle(blank:true, maxSize: 255)
```

```
            uploadedDate(nullable: true)
            displayDate(nullable: false)
            width(nullable: true)
            height(nullable: true)
            media(nullable: true, maxSize: 255)
            description(nullable: false,
                blank: false, maxSize: 2000)
            caption(nullable: true, maxSize: 2000)


    }

    static mappings = {
        cache true
    }



}
```

This class follows a similar pattern, but you will now notice the addition of a new property: hasMany. The hasMany property defines a one-to-many association to another class. It can also be used to declare a many-to-many association, as long as one side of the relationship is deemed the owner of the association (through the use of belongsTo)

The hasMany relationship works in a similar fashion to the belongsTo convention: you are defining a map in which the keys correspond to the property (that is, collection) names and the values correspond to the domain class. In our example, we are defining two associations: comments and categories. When Grails deciphers this property, it will create corresponding collections to be used to hold these associations. We can define the type of collection we would like to use by explicitly declaring the collection as a property. For instance, we define our categories association (in our ArtEntity domain class) as a java.util.Set by explicitly defining this property:

```
Set categories = new HashSet();
```

Tip   If you need to ensure that a collection is logically ordered, you can define a property of type `SortedSet` and have your collection class implement the `Comparable` interface, in which the ordering logic is specified. For instance, if we wanted our categories to be ordered alphabetically, we would have our `Category` class implement `Comparable` and define a `compareTo(def obj1, def ob2)` method in which the ordering is based on the category name.

Customizing Domain Class Hibernate Mappings

You probably noticed the static `mappings` property defined in each of our example domain classes. This field can be used to enhance the Hibernate mapping file that Grails creates and manages behind the scenes. In our example, we just assert that the domain entity be cached, using the `CacheManager` specified in the `Config.groovy` file. However, the mapping construct is extremely flexible and can be used to modify many areas of the default Hibernate mapping for a particular domain class. For instance, if you need to override the table name or the default column name or type, the mapping DSL provides a means for this to be accomplished. It is also possible to add caching rules for collections or override the default fetching policy for a collection, specifying whether a particular collection will be lazily or eagerly fetched. You can even specify that one or more columns map to a particular Hibernate `UserType`.

In our earlier Hibernate example, we defined a hierarchy of `ArtData` classes (each extended from the `ArtData` base class). In Grails, implementing polymorphic domain classes is even simpler. Here is our `ArtData` class:

```
class ArtData {
    byte[] picture;

    static mapping = {
        cache true
    }

}
```

And here is the `ArtData_Storage` class (which extends `ArtData`):

```
class ArtData_Storage extends ArtData {

}
```

That's really all there is to it. By default, Grails uses the table-per-hierarchy strategy, meaning it persists the sum of all the properties across the entire hierarchy into a single table. Unlike Hibernate, there is no need to explicitly define a discriminator (to help differentiate between types), as Grails will take care of this for us. However, Grails is flexible enough to allow us to use a different polymorphic strategy; if we are so inclined, we can use the custom mapping DSL described earlier like so:

```
static mapping = {
        tablePerHierarchy false
    }
```

Using Active Record as an Alternative to the DAO

Now that we've defined our Grails domain model, let's move on to persisting and retrieving this data. Throughout this book, you've learned how Spring simplifies the development of a persistence tier by enforcing several key design patterns, most notably the DAO, template, and facade patterns. Although Grails is built on the foundations of Spring and Hibernate, it provides an alternative to the DAO pattern typical of most Spring applications. Following the lead of other rapid development frameworks, such as Ruby on Rails, Grails utilizes the active record design pattern as the approach for handling database persistence operations.

In keeping with the active record pattern, a table in the database is represented directly by a domain class. For instance, in our gallery example, we have already defined a `Person` class that describes a corresponding `Person` table in our database, meaning table fields and associations are represented by properties within our `Person` class.

This approach doesn't seem too different from the domain models we've used throughout this book. However, the key distinction is that the domain class also serves as the wrapper around database operations. Dynamic static methods are injected into each domain class, providing a means for querying for instances of that class's type. As in Hibernate, each row in our database is represented by a corresponding instance of the appropriate domain class. However, `save()` and `update()` methods are injected into each domain class instance, allowing newly created or retrieved instances to be persisted by invoking `save()` or `update()` directly on that instance.

For example, if we want to create or update a particular row in the `Person` table, we just call `person.save()` directly on the `person` instance we wish to save. If we want to load a particular `Person` record from the database, we simply call the static method `Person.get(id)`, passing in the primary key for the record we wish to retrieve.

Contrast this approach to the DAO pattern, in which we need to create a separate abstraction layer for all database operations related to a particular domain entity. The active record pattern dramatically simplifies our effort for retrieving and persisting data, since there is no need to define any DAO classes or methods. Instead, this functionality is implicit within our domain model through dynamic behavior that is injected into each domain class.

Understanding the Active Record Pattern

If we don't need to define a DAO implementation, where do the implementations for methods like `Person.get(id)` and `Person.save()` come from? The active record pattern states that we should simply be able to define a domain model and begin calling methods on these classes to achieve the persistence logic we are trying to build. The question remains, however: if we can simply call `save()` on our `Person` instance, where do we define the behavior for this method? Let's take a look under the hood of Grails's dynamic finder implementation to get a better sense of how this works!

Looking Under the Hood of GORM

One of the key advantages to languages like Groovy is that they are dynamic, which means, among other things, that we are able to define new behavior for our classes at any time. In the case of Grails and the active record pattern, the framework is able to enhance your domain model with new functionality related to persistence. This strategy is a key Groovy concept and is enabled through the use of Groovy's `metaClass` construct.

We won't go into too much detail regarding the mechanics of how this Groovy magic works. But as a brief, cursory example, let's say we wanted to add a new method to our `Person` instance at runtime called `sayHello()`. This could be accomplished as follows:

```
Person.metaClass.sayHello = {
    println("Hello")
}
```

Or we can make this a static method that takes a single parameter:

```
Person.metaClass.static.sayHello = {def name ->
    println("hello ${name}")
}
```

In Groovy, every class holds a reference to a corresponding `metaClass`. Method calls to a particular class or instance are delegated to that class's `metaClass`, which then invokes the appropriate method. So you can think of `metaClass` as an intermediary, or proxy of sorts, allowing more of a class's behavior to be determined at runtime. By defining a new property on a particular class's `metaClass`, we are essentially implementing new behavior at runtime. In our preceding example, once we have defined our `sayHello` property to contain a closure block, future calls to `Person.sayHello()` will end up being delegated to the functionality specified in our closure block.

Note   For a given method, constructor, or property, the Groovy compiler actually generates a call to `MetaClass.invokeMethod()`, passing along the object, method name, and corresponding parameters. A Groovy object's `metaClass` can then decide what code gets invoked at runtime.

You don't need to know too much about `metaClass` to use Groovy's and Grails's dynamic features. However, I think it's important to point out a few key Groovy concepts before getting deeper into Grails development.

Getting to Know Groovy

The most fundamental difference between Grails persistence and the other approaches we've discussed in this book is that Grails is the only strategy that doesn't use Java. However, Groovy code runs in the Java Virtual Machine (JVM) and so is bytecode-compatible with Java code. Syntactically, it's very similar to Java code as well. The key difference is that Groovy is a dynamic language, which implies some significant differences both syntactically and in the way Groovy can be used.

A complete discussion on Groovy is beyond the scope of this book, however, a few core concepts are important to understand.

Letting Your Types Loose

Groovy variables and references don't need to be statically typed. For instance, you can define a variable in the following way:

```
def myName = "Paul"
```

The variable `myName` can contain a `String` or can later change to an `int`. Using `def` gives you a lot more flexibility.

Using GStrings: Strings on Steroids

Groovy supports a concept called *GStrings*, which are basically Java `Strings` on steroids. In the earlier example, notice that we were able to create a dynamic `String` by writing `"hello ${name}"`. This strategy integrates a variable directly within a `String` without requiring concatenation. You can even invoke methods directly within a `${}` block as well.

Using Default Constructors in Groovy

Another key concept is that Groovy classes can take a `Map` constructor composed of default properties. For instance, I can instantiate a Groovy class using the following approach:

```
Class GroovyBean {
    String name
    String favoriteColor
}
def myBean = new GroovyBean(
        [name: 'Paul', color: 'blue');
```

There are a few important details in the preceding example. First off, you will notice that I defined a Groovy bean without actually defining corresponding getters and setters (and without using any semicolons!). Groovy defines these for us behind the scenes. If I choose, I could reference the name property of the myBean instance with myBean.getName(). But using the more concise myBean.name is effective shorthand.

Also notice the shortcut we used for passing in a java.util.Map of bean properties. Maps can be defined using the following syntax: [key: value]. A common idiom is to define an empty map as [:].

Similarly, a java.util.List can be defined using the [] notation.

Using Closures in Groovy

One of Groovy's most significant features is its excellent support for closures. *Closures* are like methods but can also be referenced by variables or passed as parameters into methods. For instance, we can create a closure and store it in a variable called myClosure using the following code:

```
def myClosure = {param ->
   println("The param is ${param}")
}
```

Notice that closure parameters appear after the first curly brace and are then followed by ->. Closures can be used to dramatically simplify our code. For example, we can iterate through a list in Groovy this way:

```
List myList = ["a","b","c"]
myList.each {curItem ->
    println(curItem);
}
```

Contrast this approach to using a Java Iterator:

```
List myList<String> = new java.util.ArrayList();
myList.add("a"); myList.add("b"); myList.add("c");
Iterator<String> myIterator = myList.iterator();
```

```
while (myIterator.hasNext()) {
    String curItem = myIterator.next();
    System.out.print(curItem);
}
```

This is impressive, but it gets better. Imagine we wanted to iterate through a list of Strings, returning only those items that contain the sequence "cat." In Groovy, this can be accomplished quite simply:

```
def stringList = ["I like dogs",
"I like cats", "I like to scat sing",
"What is a category", "I have gas"]
def matchingStrings = stringList.findAll {curString ->
    curString.contains("cat")
}
```

Now that we've covered a few basic Groovy concepts, let's continue building our Grails persistence tier. There is a lot more to learn about Groovy, and we recommend you check out the Apress books *Beginning Groovy and Grails* by Christopher M. Judd, Joseph Faisal Nusairat, and Jim Shingler (Apress, 2008) as well as *The Definitive Guide to Grails* by Graeme Rocher (Apress, 2006).

Working with Dynamic Finder Methods

Grails injects new functionality into every domain model class to facilitate the active record pattern. Unlike the DAO approach, no methods need to be defined up front. Instead, Grails uses naming conventions to interpret how to interact with the database: using the name of the method invoked, Grails intuits what type of operation to perform. This is best explained through a few examples.

Getting back to our gallery application, let's define a simple unit test that illustrates saving and loading our Person domain class. Since we want to illustrate how Grails behaves within a running application, we need to create an integration test, which actually bootstraps a Spring ApplicationContext, so we can test functionality that relies on core

Grails features such as persistence. Grails ships with a script that creates the integration test scaffolding for us:

```
grails create-integration-test Person
```

After running this command, you will find an integration test stub under `test/integration/PersonTests.groovy`. Open this file, and remove the default method that was created. In our test, we are going to verify that we can instantiate, save, and load a `Person` domain entity:

```
class PersonTests extends GroovyTestCase {

    void testSavePerson() {

        Person person = new Person(
          [firstName: "Paul", lastName: "Fisher",
            username: "pfisher", password: "1234",
            emailAddress: "paul@notarealaddress.com",
            roleLevel: Person.ADMIN_ROLE])

        assertTrue (
          "Person entity is valid and can be saved",
          (person.validate() && person.save()))

        assertNotNull ("person id is null", person.id)

        def loadedPerson = Person.get(person.id)

        assertTrue(
          "Person was successfully loaded",
    loadedPerson != null && loadedPerson.username != null)
        }
    }
}
```

This is a very straightforward test. Notice that we instantiate our `Person` entity using a `java.util.Map` containing default properties for our Groovy class. After our `Person` instance is instantiated, we verify that the instance validates and saves successfully. `Validate()` verifies all the requirements specified within our domain model's `constraints` block. If our domain model does not validate successfully, Grails will set an `errors` property on our `Person` instance. The `errors` property contains details on each validation failure and is an implementation of the `org.springframework.validation.Errors` interface. This interface is quite useful for tracking and managing form submissions and should be familiar to users of Spring MVC.

In the event of a validation error, we can iterate through each error to find out what exactly went wrong:

```
person.errors.allErrors.each {curError ->
    log.error(
        "Error saving Person instance: ${curError}");
}
```

We can also get an error count this way:

```
person.errors.errorCount()
```

Note   A `log` instance variable is automatically injected in all `Controller` and `Service` classes, allowing you to easily emit logging messages. This is an instance of log4j's `Logger` class, and is configured in the `Config.groovy` file we described earlier in this chapter.

Grails ships with a tag library that helps to render errors within a typical form submission. Additionally, the default Grails templates will create GSP views that will automatically render clean error messages in the event of any validation or save failures. Of course, default error messages can be easily overridden by updating the `messages.properties` file.

At this point, you should have a solid understanding of how to go about saving and loading a domain entity. Unfortunately, that won't get you very far. Let's examine how we can query for a collection of objects based on a condition.

Returning to our `PersonTests.groovy` file, let's create a couple of new methods. First off, we'll define a `setup()` method that will get executed before each of our tests are run and allow us to populate the database with some sample data:

```groovy
void setUp() {
  def baseNames = [
    "Paul", "Solomon", "Heather",
    "Steve", "Sofia"]
  baseNames.each {curName ->
    def person = new Person(
      [firstName: curName,
       lastName: curName,
       username: curName,
       password: "1234",
       emailAddress: "${curName}@apress.com",
       roleLevel: Person.USER_ROLE])
    assertTrue (
      "Person entity is valid and can be saved",
      (person.validate() && person.save()))
    assertFalse(
      "There should be no errors on the saved entity",
      person.hasErrors())
  }
}
```

This method is a little archaic, as we simply iterate through a `java.util.List` of names and create new `Person` entities using these names as seed data for each field. Also notice that we've added a new assertion to verify that `person.hasErrors()` is `false`. After a `save` operation, calling `hasErrors()` is a useful idiom to ascertain that there were no errors preventing the entity from being persisted to the database. You will see this approach used frequently within the default Grails controllers.

Now that we have a way to seed our database with some sample data, let's see how Grails makes querying the database very intuitive:

```
void testFinders() {
  def foundPeople = Person. ➥
                    findAllByUsername("Paul");
  /* foundPeople should reference a List
     containing one Person entity */
  assertEquals(
    "One person found", 1, foundPeople.size())
  /* singlePerson should refer to a single Person
     entity, and the lastName property
     should be equal to Paul*/
  def singlePerson = Person.findByUsername("Paul")
  assertEquals(
    "Lastname is Paul", "Paul", singlePerson.lastName)
  def allPeopleSorted =
    Person.list(max: 3, order: "asc",
      sort: "username", offset: 0);
  assertTrue(
    "Three people returned", allPeopleSorted.size())
  assertEquals(
    "First person in list is Paul", "Paul",
    allPeopleSorted[0].username)

}
```

This new method helps to illustrate a lot of the flexibility for querying data using Grails's dynamic finder concept. You will notice that the way each method name is formatted determines the query that eventually gets generated on the database.

In our first example, we run `Person.findAllByUsername("Paul")`. This type of structure returns *all* data that matches the field `username`. Notice that we use camel casing. The format might be better expressed using the following structure:

```
DOMAIN.findAllBy<PROPERTYNAME>
```

If you look at the assertions, you will notice that this type of method will always return a collection of objects. Conversely, our next assertion uses the format:

```
DOMAIN.findBy<PROPERTYNAME>
```

This method works in a similar fashion but will return only a single object. This claim is validated on our assertion, as we demonstrate that the returned value is a single `Person` instance, instead of a collection.

Both the `findAllBy` and `findBy` dynamic methods can also be expanded further, in order to specify modifiers on the property name or provide further constraints. For example, if we wanted to find all users that have first and last names that start with the letter *p*, this could be expressed in the following method:

```
Person.findAllByFirstNameIlikeAndLastNameIlike(
                            "P%", "P%");
```

In the preceding example, we first specified a conditional property of `firstName` and then modified the condition using `Ilike`. The `Ilike` modifier is similar to the `like` modifier but is case insensitive. Next, we append `And` to the method name to further constrain the query with an additional property condition. It is also important to point out that a similar approach may be taken to find out the number of rows in the database that match a specified set of conditions by using the `countBy*` dynamic finder method.

Based on this example, we can define a method-naming structure that delineates the way in which a dynamic-finder method is formatted:

```
countBy/findBy/findAllBy<PROPERTYNAME><MODIFIER> ↪
                AND/OR<PROPERTYNAME><MODIFIER>
```

A partial list of modifiers that can be used follows:

- Between
- GreaterThan
- GreaterThanEquals
- LessThan
- LessThanEquals
- Like
- Ilike
- Not
- Equal

Our next example simply calls `Person.list()`, which returns all the instances of the `Person` domain class. However, we also pass in a `Map` of options that help to define constraints and sorting options on our returned data. These options can also be used for pagination, since we can set the maximum number of items to return, `max`, as well as an `offset`. Table 8-1 summarizes the options that can be passed to the `list()` method:

Table 8-1. Options for sorting and paginating a result set

OPTION NAME	PURPOSE
sort	Field to sort on
order	Direction of sort (ascending or descending)
max	Maximum number of items to return
offset	Offset within total result set for first item returned

A `Map` containing the options listed in Table 8-1 will also work with the `findAllBy*` methods. For instance, we could request the second page (assuming each page contains ten objects) of `Person` instances, sorted by name in descending order:

```
def people = Person.list(
    sort: "name", order: "desc", max: 10, offset: 10);
```

Creating Advanced Query Methods

Using the dynamic finder approach illustrated in the previous section, you should have the capability to define most types of queries. However, sometimes, having a little more flexibility is important. Grails also provides the find() and findAll() methods, which allow you to utilize arbitrary Hibernate Query Language (HQL) queries. Find() returns a single entity, whereas findAll() will return multiple entities. Alternatively, there is also an even more flexible executeQuery() method that allows you to define queries that don't return a specific domain entity.

Let's look at an example using HQL. Suppose we want to query for all ArtEntity objects that fall within a particular Category. This could be represented using the following query:

```
List artEntities = ArtEntity.findAll(
  "from ArtEntity artEntity left join ⮥
   artEntity.categories as category with ⮥
   category.id = :categoryId",
     ["categoryId": category.id])
```

Notice that we use a left join on the Category domain object, specifying a with constraint for those categories matching the specified category id. In the preceding example, we use named parameters in our query. As in a typical HQL query, parameter names are represented in the query by prefixing the name with a colon. The parameter name-value mappings are then passed in as a Map (as the second parameter to the findAll query).

Using the Criteria API

Just like standard Hibernate, Grails provides a means to express queries using the Criteria API. However, because we are using Groovy instead of Java, we can take advantage of a Criteria DSL, allowing us to define our query criteria in a more concise and readable way. For instance, we could query for all `ArtEntity` instances within one of two specified categories that also fall within a particular date range using the following query:

```
def criteria = ArtEntity.createCriteria()
def currentDate = new Date()
def earlierDate = currentDate - 3
def catName1 = "autumnPicts"
def catName2 = "summerPicts"
def results = criteria.list {
    between('displayDate', earlierDate, currentDate)
    categories {
        or {
            equals("name", catName1)
           equals("name", catName2)
        }
    }
}
```

The preceding example uses the Grails Criteria Builder, allowing us to express a fairly complex set of restrictions in a very intuitive manner. If you recall the standard Hibernate Criteria API, you should be able to infer most of what is occurring in our example. Criteria `Disjunctions` and `Conjunctions` can be specified using `or` or `and` blocks respectively. Similarly, association criteria may be expressed by defining a block with the association name, which is what our `categories` block does in the preceding example. Within our `categories` block is a nested `or` disjunction, and within that block are our `equals` restrictions, allowing us to filter those categories that match either of the category names we've specified. To review HQL or the Hibernate Criteria API, please refer to Chapter 3, or take a look at the Hibernate documentation.

Handling Associations in Grails

We have described how associations can be defined by using the `hasMany` and `belongsTo` conventions. These constructs are effective for indicating how our domain entities relate to each other. Once our domain model is defined, we need to manipulate it.

Recall that in the Hibernate world, it is important to write code to ensure that bidirectional associations are properly managed. For instance, it is common practice to define add* and remove* methods within a Hibernate domain class that ensure both ends of an association are properly set or removed. Grails helps to ensure that both sides of an association are properly referenced (or dereferenced) by providing dynamic addTo* and removeFrom* methods. For instance, if we want to add new Comment instances to an ArtEntity, we could do so using the following code:

```
def loadedArtEntity = ArtEntity.findByName(
                        "Awesome Panorama");
def loggedInUser = Person.findByUsername("pfisher");
Comment newComment = new Comment(
                        comment: "Cool pict!",
                        commentDate: new Date(),
                        person: loggedInUser);
loadedArtEntity.addToComments(newComment);
if (!loadedArtEntity.hasErrors() &&
                loadedArtEntity.save()) {
    println("new comment saved");
} else {
    println("Error saving new comment");
}
```

In our example, we define a new Comment and add it to the ArtEntity comments association using the addToComments method. We could also choose to remove a particular comment reference using the removeFromComments method. Notice that we did not invoke save() on our new Comment instance directly. Instead, we saved our ArtEntity instance, allowing the save operation to cascade to the comments association, since we have specified that ArtEntity is the owner of the association. This association ownership is expressed in this line within the Comment domain class:

```
static belongsTo = [commentedArt: ArtEntity]
```

Scaffolding Your Grails Application

Discussing all facets of Grails development is beyond the scope of this book, so we won't get into too much detail about building controllers and GSPs. These details can be found in *The Definitive Guide to Grails*. However, with our domain model defined, we can rely on Grails's generation scripts to create scaffolded functionality for our gallery application. You can download the full Grails-based gallery application from this book's page on the Apress web site.

To generate controllers and views for a particular domain class, make sure you are at the root of our Grails gallery application and then run

```
grails generate-all <<domain-class>>
```

Be sure to swap `domain-class` for the name of the domain entity for which you would like to generate controllers and GSPs. You can also generate just the controllers or just the GSPs by calling the following scripts, respectively:

```
Grails generate-controller <<domain-class>
Grails generate-views <<domain-class>>
```

We strongly recommend examining the generated controllers and views to get a better sense of how a typical Grails application works. Keep in mind that the generated code is based on scaffolding designed to work in a very generic way (so that it works for all types of domain models). Therefore, it is also useful to examine the sample Grails gallery application for a slightly different perspective.

Building and Running Your Application

You can easily start-up your Grails application using a particular
environment by passing the `grails.env` environment variable into the
`grails run-app` script:

```
grails -Dgrails.env=development run-app
```

This command will automatically start up our application using the
`development` environment configuration. We wouldn't normally want to
run our production or staging application this way, but it is rather
convenient for testing purposes. Internally, Grails uses an embedded Jetty
server to run your application when you use the `run-app` command.

You can deploy Grails to any application server if you create a WAR file
using the Grails `war` command. If you want to create an application for
deploying into your own application server, you would instead run this:

```
grails -Dgrails.env=production war
```

We recommend explicitly using `-Dgrails.env` to specify an environment,
as it supports both default and custom environments. However, if you are
using the default Grails environments, you can use this shortcut:

```
grails prod war
```

Defining a Transactional Service Layer in Grails

You've learned about transactional support throughout this book and know
how important it is to ensure that operations within a particular method all
complete (or roll back) as a single, atomic unit of work. Grails also
encourages the use of the service facade pattern and makes defining
transactional requirements extremely easy. However, in the name of
flexibility, Grails provides a couple of options for ensuring persistent
operations occur within a transactional context.

If you don't want to create a service class, an alternative approach for ensuring persistence operations occur within a transactional context is to enclose a block of code inside a closure and pass this to the dynamic withTransaction method, injected to each domain class. For instance, we could ensure an update to a category and an ArtEntity occur within a transaction by doing the following:

```
Comment.withTransaction {txStatus ->
    def comments = Comment.
        findAllByCommentDateGreaterThan(lastWeek);
    comments.each {Comment curComment ->
      if (Comment.hasSpam(curComment)) {
        curComment.delete()
      }
    }
}
```

In the preceding example, we are actually defining an anonymous closure block and passing this closure to the Comment domain object's dynamic withTransaction method. This is a trivial example, but it illustrates how simple defining a transaction can be using Grails.

Note   The txStatus closure parameter is an org.springframework .transaction.TransactionStatus object that allows you to get information about the currently executing transaction and programmatically trigger a rollback by calling txStatus.setRollbackOnly().

Generating a Service Class

A cleaner approach, however, is to implement a service layer and organize your transactional operations within a service method. In Grails, we can create a new service method by running the following command:

```
grails create-service servicename
```

This will create a new service within the `grails-app/services` directory. Grails has a fairly simplistic way of declaring whether a particular service class should be transactional. Simply add the following to the top of your service class:

```
static transacational = true;
```

If `transactional` is set to `true`, our methods will all run within a transactional context. If the static property is `false`, a transaction will not be used.

Summary

In this chapter, you've learned some of the fundamentals for developing a web application using Groovy and Grails. Grails provides an interesting contrast to earlier chapters in this book: although firmly based on Spring and Hibernate, Grails utilizes the active record pattern as an alternative to the DAO design pattern. This approach is more practical in Grails because of its use of the dynamic language Groovy, and it allows new behavior and methods to be dynamically defined.

Despite some of these differences, Spring's profound influence is clearly present, and most of the lessons and patterns utilized with other persistence frameworks can still be applied to Grails. However, you've seen how Grails, through the use of convention over configuration, can significantly reduce the amount of effort required to get a working application up and running. You've also seen how some of the fundamental Spring concepts, such as dependency injection, can be further enhanced through Groovy-based configuration and implicit, convention-based wiring.

Related Titles

Fischer, Robert. *Grails Persistence with GORM and GSQL*. Berkley, CA: Apress, 2009.

Machacek, Jan, Jessica Ditt, Aleksa Vukotic, and Anirvan Chakraborty. *Pro Spring 3*. Berkley, CA: Apress, 2009.

Rocher, Graeme and Jeff Brown. *The Definitive Guide to Grails, Second Edition*. Berkley, CA: Apress, 2009.

Seddighi, Ahmad Reza. *Pro Spring Persistence with Hibernate*. Berkley, CA: Apress, 2009.

Copyright

Spring Persistence: A Running Start

© 2009 by Paul Tepper Fisher and Solomon Duskis

ISBN-13 (electronic): 978-1-4302-1878-4

ISBN-13 (paperback): 978-1-4302-1877-7

Trademarked names may appear in this book. Rather than use a trademark symbol with every occurrence of a trademarked name, we use the names only in an editorial fashion and to the benefit of the trademark owner, with no intention of infringement of the trademark.

Java™ and all Java-based marks are trademarks or registered trademarks of Sun Microsystems, Inc., in the United States and other countries. Apress, Inc., is not affiliated with Sun Microsystems, Inc., and this book was written without endorsement from Sun Microsystems, Inc.

Distributed to the book trade in the United States by Springer-Verlag New York, Inc., 233 Spring Street, 6th Floor, New York, NY 10013, and outside the United States by Springer-Verlag GmbH & Co. KG, Tiergartenstr. 17, 69112 Heidelberg, Germany.

In the United States: phone 1-800-SPRINGER, fax 201-348-4505, e-mail orders@springer-ny.com, or visit http://www.springer-ny.com. Outside the United States: fax +49 6221 345229, e-mail orders@springer.de, or visit http://www.springer.de.

For information on translations, please contact Apress directly at 2855 Telegraph Ave, Suite 600, Berkeley, CA 94705. Phone 510-549-5930, fax 510-549-5939, e-mail info@apress.com, or visit http://www.apress.com.

Breinigsville, PA USA
18 February 2011

255834BV00005B/16/P

9 781430 218777